AF076424

THE ROAD TO RECOVERY

The Lean Years

THE ROAD TO RECOVERY

The Lean Years

JOHN D. CADORE

The Road to Recovery
Copyright © 2022 by John D. Cadore. All rights reserved.

No part of this publication may be reproduced, stored in a retrieval system or transmitted in any way by any means, electronic, mechanical, photocopy, recording or otherwise without the prior permission of the author except as provided by USA copyright law.

The opinions expressed by the author are not necessarily those of URLink Print and Media.

1603 Capitol Ave., Suite 310 Cheyenne, Wyoming USA 82001
1-888-980-6523 | admin@urlinkpublishing.com

URLink Print and Media is committed to excellence in the publishing industry.

Book design copyright © 2022 by URLink Print and Media. All rights reserved.

Published in the United States of America

Library of Congress Control Number: 2022906897
ISBN 978-1-68486-167-5 (Paperback)
ISBN 978-1-68486-168-2 (Digital)

10.03.22

DEDICATION

This book is dedicated in loving memory of my sister, Gladys Emilda Cadore-Williams, AKA, Ivy Cadore who passed away at the young age of 62, on April 10, 2020, with complications from Covid - 19.

Ivy was my best friend and confidant. Simply stated, she was the rock that kept me anchored: She encouraged and supported me in all my endeavors and corrected me when necessary.

Ivy was relentless in her giving to others and cared not just for family, which included her three lovely sons, and friends, but for everyone. She wanted to make the world a better place and to that end she contributed selflessly.

Ivy served in the U.S. Army (active duty) for eight years before joining the Army Reserves Medical Corps where she retired at the rank of Lieutenant Colonel. She was a Registered Nurse and served as a Senior Manager with the New York City Metropolitan Transit Authority, with responsibility for all of the assessment centers to include Brooklyn, Queens and Staten Island. With all of those responsibilities, Ivy still found time to serve as President of the Grenada, Carriacou and Petit Martinique Nurses Association, and as President of the Lions Club International, District 20-K1, one of the branches of the world's largest service club organization.

Additionally, Ivy served as Chairperson and/or Co-Chair on more than eleven other Committees in District 20-K1. The word "NO" was not in Ivy's vocabulary. Her favorite words were, "What can I help with?"

Ivy was also one of the Founding members of the Maylive Frederick Public Library, a Resource Center in the Parish of St. Marks, Grenada, West Indies, and a member of Hands Across the World, an organization which assists the less fortunate. This organization helps the less fortunate children in two schools in Ghana, West Africa. She sponsored less fortunate children by paying their yearly tuition fees, at the time of her passing she was the proud sponsor of four Ghanaian children.

Ivy worked tirelessly, helping others in her attempt to make the world a better place to live in. The kindness she showed to others and the many lives she had touched are what make it easier to accept that she is no longer with us. A humble sole she was, always shying away from accolades; although she received numerous awards. What mattered most to Ivy was knowing that she made a difference in the lives of many.

It is said that 'only the good die young', in Ivy's case, this saying is truly meritorious. Ivy left us too soon, but the work she did while here on earth will last many lifetimes, and as for her memories, they will forever remain in our hearts.

THE ROAD TO RECOVERY

CHAPTER 1

STARTING OVER AFTER DEFAMATION, LIBEL, AND SLANDER

At that point of my life, I envisioned early retirement, not starting over. It is so true; the future is a complete unknown. Starting over is something that was never thought of or even envisioned. However, this is now my new reality.

Restarting my practice after my name has been wrongly disgraced and my character wrongly assassinated is a challenge worth undertaking. It's my opinion that the biggest test would be to regain the public trust and confidence. This, I believe, would be accomplished within my first two years of returning to practice. I say returning to practice because during the years of my ordeal, my focus was switched from practicing law to writing and publishing books. I wrote three books within that time period, and my intention is to continue writing books for the foreseeable future.

December 4, 2016 – A Day of Coincidence

Today, December 4, 2016, was my first full day back in my downtown law office since October 11, 2012, the day that New York State Attorney General's Office secured a warrant to confiscate three hundred and forty-four of my clients' files. Today was mostly spent making phone calls to various court offices in Broome County, Tioga County, and Delaware County informing them that my office is once again open for business. I also received one phone call from a former client. However, the bulk of my time at the office was spent making phone calls to various courts and writing follow-up letters.

Today, December 4, 2016 is coincidentally the thirty-sixth anniversary of my enlistment in the U.S army. I departed from Fort Hamilton, New York on the 4th of December 1979, for basic training at Fort Leonard Wood, Missouri. My recollection is that a group of enlistees departed from Fort Hamilton, New York on the 4th of December 1979 at about 6:30 a.m. and arrived at Fort Leonard Wood Missouri at about midnight on that day. This marked the start of my military career - a career in which I served in the U.S Army, the U.S Army Reserves, the Texas Army National Guard, the New York Army National Guard, and a period in the Ready Reserves.

This day thirty-six years ago reminds me of a new beginning, whereas today it's a second start of my law practice. This, however, was not as planned; it just happened. What a coincidence. Where do I go from here?

CHAPTER 2

WHAT WOULD I HAVE DONE DIFFERENTLY?

The biggest thing I would have done differently is spending less time at the office (at work) and more time with my family. A job, a profession, or an occupation is very important because it allows one to put food on his or her family's table, pay his or her mortgage, and send his or her children to school or university. However, it is my belief that spending time – quality time – with one's family is of tremendous importance and is an invaluable commodity. After all, how valuable would one's life be if all one has ever done is work long hours and accumulate worldly possessions? My answer to this question is that life would be meaningless.

CHAPTER 3

FEBRUARY 10TH, 2016 – A SLIGHT SEMBLANCE OF NORMALITY

Upon returning to my law office on the 5th of January 2016 - an office I occupied since May 2006, there was a slight return to normalcy. Of course, I never stopped the practice of Law, but today – the 10th of February – I received a letter from the County of Tioga, New York inquiring about the areas of law and different courts in which I would like to serve. Compared to where I left of on the 11th of October 2012, when I had approximately one hundred and fifty open files (cases),this is a step back to normalcy or in the right direction. Since October 11, 2012, the day that three hundred and forty-four of my clients' files were seized from my office, my legal practice had significantly declined. My significantly reduced caseload, together with my loss of motivation to practice law, resulted in me being virtually unemployed. A significant factor in being a successful attorney is one's credibility. It is my belief that whenever there are criminal charges pending or any significant negative event involving an attorney until and unless a positive resolution is reached, there exists a shadow of doubt on the issue of credibility. It's my opinion that credibility is always an issue. The credibility and reputation of both the attorney and the litigants are always an issue in every case.

The Feeling of Optimism

Today, there is a strong feeling of optimism in the environment. A feeling that is hard to describe.

But a feeling that restoration is (at hand) near. It is very difficult and sometimes unbearable to fall down, but it is also very rewarding and comforting to get back up. It's my belief that recovering after being knocked down is at least ten times more rewarding than having success without ever falling down. True self- gratification and the feeling of accomplishment is much more pronounced and enjoyable when one recovers from being knocked down. Although it's very painful to be knocked down, in hindsight being knocked down is good because it builds perseverance and character. As condescending, phony, or sad as it might sound, being knocked down is not bad at all. It refocuses you and helps to rearrange one's priorities. Most importantly, it quickly allows you to discern what's worthwhile from what is not. There is some truth to the saying that time heals all wounds and what doesn't kill you will make you stronger.

CHAPTER 4

MY FINANCIAL PROBLEMS AND HARDSHIPS

The biggest impediment to recovery is one's financial matters. Loss of employment and income can have a significant negative effect on one's credit. Today- September 8, 2016- has been a roller coaster of a day. Next month, October 23, 2016 to be exact, would be one year since I was victorious in all my legal matters. However, my financial situation persisted. Just at the moment when I am convinced that I have turned the corner and that my bad days are behind me, there comes an incident to dampen my bright hopes.

Today I went to the court in a Code Enforcement matter. A matter which was due to a children play pen and other indoor/outdoor furniture owned by one of my tenant's. That play pen is utilized by the tenant's children for their relaxation, fun and entertainment. The Code Enforcement Officer viewed the tenant's belongings as garbage, when in fact the tenant saw it as very important and valuable. This reminded me of an age old saying: one man's garbage is another man's treasure.

However, to make a bad day worse, at about 6:00 p.m. I received a summons and complaint from a credit card company threatening to seek a judgment for an unpaid bill. My first reaction was one of discontent. Then, I had to remind myself that like every other bad or unexpected situation, this too will soon be over, and I would be handling it to the best of my ability. This matter was dismissed.

For individuals that have never been through major law suits, particularly a defendant in a serious legal matter, it can take both an emotional and financial toll. This experience can be further complicated when one is innocent of all charges and is innocent of everything one is being accused of.

CHAPTER 5

MY LAW SUIT AGAINST THE BROOME COUNTY AND THE STATE OF NEW YORK.

Today – the 25th of April 2016 – approximately one year and three months after the acquittal of all charges against me, I took significant steps towards partial recovery of all that was wrongfully, unjustly, and intentionally taken away from me by people with political agendas. There is an old saying what goes around comes around. My father who is currently ninety-nine years of age has added to this old saying by adding, "One would be rather surprised at the speed at which things come around".

To capitalize on my father's saying, it goes like this, "What goes around comes around with lightning speed". My father's saying, in my case, has already proven itself to be true. The two-term Broome County Executive, Debbie Preston, who according to sources was one of the people instrumental in the events leading up to my accusal, was recently indicted on three counts of "official misconduct, and plead guilty to one of those counts". According to the Special

Prosecutor- Schuyler County district attorney- Debbie Preston unlawfully obtained a credit card in her name and wrongfully spent more than $ 20,000. According to reliable sources, it has to do with spending of public funds or using an official credit card during a period after she was no longer working in that capacity. In her case, she was the town supervisor of a small town. She unlawfully obtained the credit card in her name and in the name of the municipality, where she was once the town supervisor.

According to reliable sources, in exchange for her guilty plea, Preston paid a $1,000 fine and did not receive any jail time. Reliable sources revealed that Preston is or was trying to shift blame by claiming that the case required a special prosecutor from outside Broome County because of threats she received from District Attorney Steve Cornwell.

The District Attorney's Office later released a statement saying, "Debra Preston's guilty plea, despite her changing story, confirms what our investigation concluded: She is guilty of violating the public trust". According to Preston, "No one should be afraid of the justice system, but I have to say that I am, because of all that I've gone through".

This is ironic; these are the same people that earlier accused me of over-billing the county and state of roughly ($10,000.00) ten thousand dollars for legal work performed. Isn't that ironic? Or, is it poetic justice? My ninety-nine-year old father, soon to be one hundred years old, has repeatedly told me that 'when the final bell tolls in my case, I would be surprised at how well my outcome would be'. He frequently reminds me that his father, my grandfather, was once involved in a law suit for seven years. According to my father, when my grandfather's case was finally over, it was a total and complete victory for him. My grandfather got better results than he was expecting. According to my father, my final outcome would be even better than that of my grandfather's.

Now back to my civil action against the County of Broome and the State of New York, it is not wise to comment on ongoing litigation. However, litigation is currently ongoing against the County of Broome and the state of New York.

The former two-term Broome County Executive began this trouble by promising the voters that she would go after the "highest paid lawyers that perform legal duties for the county". Like most other politicians, she was making promises to address issues that she knew nothing about. As some people would say, "Power went to her head, and she became power-hungry." Had she known the vast number of hours worked and the vast number of cases involved, just maybe she would've been a little smarter. Although I am now primarily focusing on the merits of the case, it's my sincere belief that "race", being an African American immigrant attorney, played a significant role in the treatment I received. I believe that race would also play a significant part in how this civil action against Broome County and the State of New York will proceed and in the outcome of the case.

CHAPTER 6

DECEPTION AND DECEPTIVE PRACTICES OF NEW YORK STATE ATTORNEY GENERAL'S OFFICE

Although this book is entitled *Road to Recovery: The Lean Years*, it is somewhat impossible to overlook the dishonesty and deceptive practices utilized by the New York State Attorney General's Office in my case in order to secure a conviction. Today, as I listen to the news of the State of Arkansas' execution of inmates by lethal injection, I can't help but ask myself how many of those men that were put to death this week and the coming weeks were and are innocent? How many of those men were found guilty because of lies and deceptive tactics used by the prosecutors seeking to further their careers? How many of those men were convicted because of ineffective assistance and poor counsel? My encounter as a defendant in the legal system has vastly opened my eyes to many irregularities and uses of words that, if not properly addressed, can lead to wrongful accusations.

Let's use my case as an example. One of the allegations against me was that I billed a total of $747,139.00 from January 1, 2009 through September 30, 2011. By making that statement, the prosecutor knowingly, intentionally, and maliciously lied to the Court and the jury in order to prove their case. The prosecutors know that some of the cases billed in 2009, 2010, and 2011 were assigned in the years 2006, 2007, 2008, 2009, 2010, and 2011. Most shockingly, the prosecutors knew that many of the cases billed between the years 2009 and 2011 were completed in the years 2006, 2007, 2008, 2009, 2010, and 2011 and were billed in some instances several years later. For example, many cases billed in 2009 were actually completed in the years 2006, 2007, and 2008. In fact, about one -half of the cases billed in 2009 were assigned and completed in years prior to 2009. One may ask how rampant is such deception within the New York State Attorney General's Office and state and local prosecutor's offices throughout the country.

My experience has led me to believe that these types of deceptive practices are very common. I believe one reason for such prosecutorial deception is because prosecutors are trying to climb the legal ladder and the social ladder. And in many cases, it is done by any means necessary. In the case of the New York State Attorney General, it's my belief that his eyes are set on the New York State gubernatorial race, and maybe sometime in the future, the presidency of the United States. He has learned that maybe one of the fastest ways to accomplish his goals is to use whatever means are necessary -which would include the destruction of some peoples' professional reputations and careers - in order to build his own.

How would the prosecutors know that accusing me of billing $747,139.00 from January 1, 2009 to September 30, 2011 is false?

This is a question that would be asked by numerous individuals who have read the book. The answer to this question is that on every case, in order to be paid, one must submit a voucher. On each voucher, the attorney must include the date the case was assigned and the date it was completed. Therefore, the state accountants and prosecutors had all of the evidence in front of them but decided to take the low road. They did so because taking the low road would get them more expeditiously to their final intended destination - a position of power and improved social standing.

As I am writing this part of my book, I am seriously debating whether it would be important to release the actual breakdown of the cases assigned, completed, and billed from 2006 through September 30, 2011. Relevant questions taken into consideration are: would making the number of cases assigned, completed, and billed from January 1, 2009 to September 30, 2011 be too personal? Will it be too tedious, thus causing readers to lose interest, and would it make a significant contribution to this book? I am currently weighing all options before a conclusion is reached.

My goal throughout my tenure as an attorney was always to, first, provide good service. This still is my most important goal. Billing was never my top priority or first priority. That's the reason why some cases completed in 2006 were billed in 2009. This was a very common occurrence throughout my legal practice. My motto is that good service would bring money and clients not vice versa. That is the reason why I was so amazed when accusations of fraudulent behavior and practices were levied against me.

CHAPTER 7

LIVING FROM ONE PAY CHECK TO ANOTHER OR FROM PAY CHECK TO PAY CHECK

This chapter entitled Living from One Pay Check to Another – or From Pay Check to Pay Check reminds me vividly of my days as an undergraduate student, a graduate student, a law student, and as a doctoral student. I can remember vividly during my university days going into the grocery store to do my grocery shopping, and having to first look at the prices of all items and compare them, and then putting the cheapest item into my grocery cart. For about one decade, this was a normal and routine part of my life. I had gotten used to it.

However, after practicing law for about two years, I eventually relinquished those habits when my financial standing began to improve, or I should say, greatly improved. After about one decade of financial prosperity and some financial affluence somehow, I had grown to forget my lean college and university years. Never believing or thinking that maybe, just maybe,

I may once again have to be a very careful or stingy shopper. Although we often hear the saying prepare for the rainy days, one never really believes that there will be lots or continuous rainy days. For example, in my case, it has been raining for over four years. However, I must say that I was not totally unprepared for the rainy days because I made many long-term and short-term investments during my sunny days. However, no matter how prepared one is for the rainy days, losing an average annual income in the six figures will have an effect.

If one should talk to my ninety-nine-year old father, soon to be one-hundred in May of 2017, about my situation, one would leave with the impression that everything is just fine and that there is nothing that I should be worried about. Despite my financial losses from the last four years, my father is of the belief that everything is fine and that I would not only be better off when it's all over, but I would eventually be thanking God that this situation occurred. According to my father, I have made many solid investments and that, despite everything, I am still very well- off.

It's my opinion that I could have done much better, and there are still lots more to be accomplished. Today, my biggest problem is to constantly have to prioritize and make choices as to what items I must purchase immediately, and what should be forgone for another day. Unfortunately, this also occurs in the paying of bills. Although I still have a monthly source of income, it's not close to what I had grown accustomed to over the past decade.

Every student of economics is taught about the notion of scarcity and choice in Economics 101. I am now of the belief that although many people are not familiar with those intellectual terms, they are very well versed in those principles learned from the school of life or from the school of hard knocks. Some people may call it the school of hard knocks. It has long been said and recognized that low- income mothers are the best economists. Their teacher is called real life. Low income stay -at- home mothers in the vast majority of instances have learned their economics lessons very well. They are the real teachers. They are also the real doctors. Thus, they should be called Dr. Mom.

The most significant aspect of experiencing reduced income is not being able to provide for your family in the way you would like to. Having to forgo some things such as family vacations and other family events. Hindsight is always twenty-twenty. However, my biggest regret is that I spend too much time at work, in my office, and not enough time with my family. My children are now attending university, one is studying accounting and intends to attend law school, and the other is studying biomedical engineering and intends to attend medical school.

My future promise is to work less and enjoy my family much more. That would entail taking more trips to the Caribbean, Canada, and maybe England. I have never been to England, but I have lots of blood relatives there. In fact, I was born in a British Colony, which I believe conferred British citizenship to me.

CHAPTER 8

MAY 5, 2017

May 5, 2017 was a day I would never forget. It was the day that encompassed all of my efforts and heartbreak of false allegations being made against me by people seeking to advance their political careers. After being victorious at trial, I made all possible attempts to resume my life as similar as possible to what it was prior to the trial. However, this was not without many difficulties. The architects of the false charges being brought against me in a court of law simply would not accept that they were wrong and that I was innocent of all the charges.

Unfortunately or fortunately, depending on where you stand on the issue, I was left with no realistic choice but to file a law suit against them. There is an old proverb that says that where one stands depends on where they are sitting or to be simply put, where one stands depends on where they sit. In my experience, this saying couldn't possibly be closer to the truth. It's my realization that the state and county employees responsible for my wrongful dilemma cannot not accept the reality of things because it will communicate to bystanders or to the public at large that they are vindictive and incompetent at their jobs.

This stubbornness of refusing to accept the truth and reality has left me with no choice but to file a civil lawsuit against the State of New York. The law suit attributes seventeen counts of wrongdoing against me by the State of New York. The three most serious counts are the ones alleging that the State of New York and the County of Broome committed libel, slander, and defamation of character against the plaintiff.

The Effects of Slander, Libel, and Defamation of Character in General

All of the above- slander, libel, and defamation of character- can serve to weaken or lessen one's ability to defend themselves. It does so in many ways. First, because character is always an issue in any situation or transaction, and second because there are those people that would not be willing to give individuals, whose character has been defamed, the benefit of the doubt. In my case, even after being fully exonerated, professionally I am currently being denied the rightful privilege of being made whole.

There is also an upside to this situation. One of the most significant advantages or upsides to experiencing slander, libel, and defamation of character is that individuals experiencing those situations would frequently reach out to you for advice and assistance. In times of trouble, human nature is usually to turn to others that had similar experiences for guidance and assistance to get through those times. The downside is that some people may become withdrawn and may not be inclined to get involved in the affairs of others. This mostly may be the case in situations where the individual may have been wrongfully accused.

It is my opinion that one's ability to get involved or give counsel to others going through periods of hardship would depend on the nature of that person whose advice is being sought and by the manner they were treated by members of society during their own periods of hard or trying times. When I say "the nature of that person", I am referring to their character traits. Some people are extroverts and others are introverts. Introverts, generally, would prefer not to get involved or if they do, it would be somewhat minimal or trivial in nature, whereas extroverts tend to be more joviall in nature and tend to be always open and ready to get involve.

CHAPTER 9

THE ARTIFICIAL NATURE OF FRIENDSHIP

My experience over the last four and a half years has exposed the depth of friendship in this society. I say this society because it would be too much of a generalization to include all cultures and nationalities. Friendship is mostly one event away from disappearing. In short, good and prosperous times would get one many friends, but the opposite is also true during hard and bad times. During troubled times, your friend is someone you talk to whenever they are encountered in the street, on your way to work, or in the work place.

There are also people that would use one's hard times to gain an upper hand for themselves or to engage in slanderous activities. In short, in times of trouble, friends are a rare commodity. Although I am not wishing troubled or hard times on anyone, it's my belief that everyone should experience it. It is a mechanism for real personal growth. It's my belief that hard or trying times may either make you, or it can break you. That depends on the person and on how they handle and react to the situation. In difficult times, friends would be very few, so it's always important to have a reliable person or persons, in my case, to talk to and have discussions with. My hundred year old father was the person that primarily kept me and my family strong throughout my ordeal. He resides in the Caribbean, so modern technology can be a true blessing.

CHAPTER 10

WHY DO SO MANY PEOPLE LACK A BACKBONE?

Although it is true that the average human being has 206 bones in their body and 33 vertebrae in their spine, it is shocking to know that few people actually have much of a real back bone. The word "backbone" when used in this chapter refers to the ability to stand up for oneself in the face of tremendous pressure and against the odds. And, in many cases, the ability to stand up to individuals in powerful places.

Conventional wisdom is that most lawyers have backbones, but my interaction with many has led me to believe the contrary. Many attorneys, although they may be excellent and tough when representing their clients, are somewhat deficient when they have to stand up for themselves.

Very shocking to me is that instead of standing up for themselves, many lawyers would prefer to find a way to attain some degree of closure or settlement. Hence, avoiding a trial where the accuser, in a criminal matter, would have to prove one's case beyond a reasonable doubt. This may be good or advantageous in some situations but in the long run, such attitudes can be more harmful than helpful. In other words, in the long run the cost may outweigh the benefits. However, I do understand the reasoning behind plea bargaining, and it can be logical in many instances. In some cases, justice can only be done by taking a case to trial.

The purpose of plea bargaining is the quick disposal of cases in an attempt to prevent back log of cases in the legal or justice system. However in many instances, justice cannot be achieved through plea bargaining. In those instances, the defendant deserves his day in court.

It was recently brought to my attention that my victory in my case was a win for the local bar association. I must confess that it was never my intention to confer any such benefits to the local bar association. My attitude towards the organization could be primarily because, throughout my ordeal, I was never supported by it.

It was expressed by many, some of whom are attorneys, that my lack of support from the local bar was primarily because of professional jealousy. To this, the question I frequently asked myself is: why be jealous of anyone? It was also expressed by many individuals that one reason for professional jealousy towards me was because I was earning more than a vast majority of my peers. There is no secret to the formula for making money. The formula for being successful financially is good service and hardwork. To me, the main ingredient for financial success is going to work early, and working late hours.

The underlying principle for being happy in one's profession or in layman's term, is liking your job and what you do. It's my belief that one should not choose their profession because of financial rewards. The naked truth is that financial rewards can be attained in any profession, but the key ingredient is liking and being happy with your profession. Liking one's profession would not only yield financial prosperity but also professional happiness and job fulfillment.

Within the world of economics and world politics, it is a well -established principle that Five percent (5%) of the people in the world lead the remaining Ninety five (95%). In the vast majority of instances, this is possible because 5% of the world owns 95% of the world's resources.

In the world of real life, only about 5% of the people in this world have the strength and self- confidence to stand up for themselves when faced with tremendous odds.

The 2016 video tape controversy with then Presidential Candidate Donald Trump and the Entertainment Tonight worker Billy Bush provides us with a prime example of what can occur when individuals lack backbone. Billy Bush, after being fired from his job for this same incident, recently addressed his deep regrets for participating in such actions, and said that his best course of action would have been to change the conversation, but he lacked the self-confidence to do so.

Why do so many people lack confidence in themselves? To me, it's much better to lead than to fit in. What level of self-fulfillment can be achieved by fitting in? Is lack of backbone hereditary or is it a learned behavior? Or is it a combination of both factors? Just imagine if the early abolitionists of slavery were content with fitting in, slavery would still be the law of the land in many countries. Imagine if Rosa Parks and Martin Luther King were content with sitting at the back of the bus, then many people of color would still be sitting in the back of the bus today. There are many instances where one has to stand up despite the consequences. Failure to do so is more than mere dereliction of duty. It is a morale and ethical failing.

CHAPTER 11

LETTERS OF RECOMMENDATION

I can recall asking two of my colleagues for a letter of recommendation in order to seek certain job opportunities. It's also my recollection that I wanted the letters of recommendation prior to my trial. Although neither of them actually refused to write them, they made excuses or gave reasons why they were unable to write the recommendations. This reminds me of the old saying that success has many fathers, but failure is an orphan. However, in my case, I knew that I was on the right side of things, the winning side, and it would only be a matter of time before the truth is finally revealed.

There is an old army saying, "The best person to ask about the army is an army private." Based on my recent experiences, I believe that this old army saying is absolutely correct. This is correct because individuals tend to reveal their true selves to the people they believe are unable to be of assistance to them in their quest to climb the social ladder. There is usually no hypocrisy and false pretense involved in such interactions and transactions.

Another question I was very frequently asked is whether I would remain in Broome County? The answer to that question is why not remain in Broome County? I am absolutely certain that many other individuals were also wrongfully accused. The deciding factor is how those individuals dealt with the hand which they were dealt. The deciding factor of life is not what happens to you but is how one reacts to what happens to them. Jesus never promised us a life free of worries and troubles; however, what he promised us is that He would always be with us throughout our troubles. Jesus himself experienced the ultimate betrayal, hence the real issue here is if Jesus the Alpha and Omega, the creator of the world was wrongfully accused and condemned, why should we be surprised when it happens to us? After all, we should all seek to become disciples of Christ.

Very recently, an individual shared or expressed a different viewpoint on my circumstance. A viewpoint that never crossed my mind, and, obviously, one that I have never thought of. According to that individual, my success by overcoming such odds could well serve as a source of comfort to many people that are currently faced with similar situations or will in the future undergo similar circumstances. That person suggested that I become visible in society so that certain individuals would be able to draw strength from me. However, that person also suggested that my silence is also conveying a very strong message and that by either being very active and visible or by being silent, people are drawing strength from me when dealing with very difficult situations.

I can vividly recall an individual that was faced with a situation somewhat similar to mine telling me that the only reason why he has not given up is because of the way I handled my situation.

The irony of this story is that a former colleague, before his passing, expressed the same or similar thanks and appreciation to me. This colleague who was also facing a difficult time expressed to me that I was the reason he did not give up. According to that former colleague, on many occasions, he was tempted to give up but the thought of me emerging victorious in such a difficult situation and against all odds served as a source of strength and hope for him.

CHAPTER 12

THE MYTH OF THE LEGAL SYSTEM

Conventional wisdom is that the purpose of the legal system is the dispensation of justice. Another myth of the legal system is that justice is blind. My theory is that both of those myths are wrong. The crux of the legal system is encompassed in certain processes. Hence, once the prescribed process is followed whether or not the truth is revealed is hardly a function of the legal system. Due process and an opportunity to be heard is the backbone of the legal system. Truth is never a guaranteed factor in that process.

The legal system is loaded with process, not substance. For example, the definition of due process is notice and an opportunity to be heard. Once proper notice is given and one is given his or her day in court then the system has worked the way it was intended to. Whether or not that individual was effectively represented is another story for another day.

However, the real problem lies with when the people elected or appointed to be judges fail to uphold the oath they swore to uphold. This failure in or of the legal system is more common than most people would believe. For example, after my victory at trial, the proper thing for the judges in Broome County and the State of New York to do should have been to restore me to the position I enjoyed prior to the start of all and every legal proceeding. However, both New York State and Broome County failed to do so. By doing so, both New York State and Broome County judges violated their oaths to administer justice fairly and impartially. Their actions reflected a total and complete dereliction of their sworn oath and duty.

One of the major reasons why this is so difficult to do is because, by so doing, they are publicly recognizing that they were wrong. Admitting that they were wrong is something most people are unable to do. There are only tiny parts of any population with the courage to admit wrongdoing when they are not forced to do so. Judges and the legal system are no different.

Here I am today 12 May 2017 writing a chapter in my book about judges' misconduct. Let's talk about my educational background. I hold an associate's degree, a bachelor's degree, and a master's degree, and I have completed all requirements except my dissertation for a PhD. With all of this education and with an education background that is far more accomplished or should I say more accomplished than the vast majority of the judges both in New York State and in Broome County, they are still colluding to deny me my legal rights. For the sake of argument, let's imagine what those same judges would do to an individual with less than a high school education that they are not fond of. At the very least, I understand the system and am capable of at least representing myself in legal proceedings. However, we should not forget that the old saying, "A lawyer who represents himself has a fool for a client".

For the sake of argument, let's say that I can represent myself and have a good understanding of the workings and process of the legal system. The average individual with less than a high school education does not have, in most cases, a good grasp or working knowledge of the legal system. It is also my contention that such people routinely have bad experiences with the legal system. Where can they turn for help? To whom can they go?

My answer to these questions is, most often than not, legal aid or legal services for individuals of low income. This may mean their only means of assistance. And as we all know, most legal aid offices are overworked, understaffed, and do not have the resources to meet the burdens that are usually placed upon them. The answer to the first question is little or no justice for the poor and uneducated. In this scenario, is the legal system dispensing justice? This question is left to be answered, not by me but by each individual either based on their experience or based on their own logic. The second question is: is justice colorblind? It is my belief that for the average American, this question is easier to answer than the first question. To properly answer this question, the readers should be asking themselves, is society colorblind? If society is colorblind, then the legal system is also colorblind. Because, after all, most judges and legal practitioners are usually members of the community in which they serve. A black robe cannot change one's disposition; it only enforces it.

CHAPTER 13

LIFE AND DRAMATIC IRONY

In times of distress and difficulty, many peoples' first instinct is to turn to their local place of worship for guidance. To many people, the notion of attending church outside of a crisis or special event (funerals or marriages) is somewhat rare or unheard of. To most churchgoers of any faith, this would seem ironic. However, it is probably unheard of that members of one's own church congregation would play a key role in assassinating their character and destroying their livelihood and then return to mass on a regular basis as if nothing had happened.

Many people reading this book or this chapter may also say that this situation is not an unfamiliar story because the Maker of the universe, the Alpha and Omega was betrayed by one of His twelve disciples condemned to a certain extent, and put to death by the religious leaders of His day. According to the Bible, and I believe that I am correct, the religious leaders that were instrumental in the condemnation of our Lord Jesus Christ did so primarily because of professional and religious jealousy. Of course, Christ did not have to die; no one could have taken His life, but He died as a ransom or payment in full for the sins of man. Nothing any human being can do or accomplish is enough to secure our place in heaven. Hence, believing and confessing to our Heavenly Father are the key ingredients for obtaining eternal life. We also know that "faith without works is dead". This is a somewhat ironical statement because, although we are all sinners and have fallen short of the glory of God and "any man that says he has not sinned is a liar", being a follower of Christ means "loving one's neighbor as him or herself". This is one aspect of the golden rule: do unto others as you would like them to do unto you. Anyone that adheres to this principle is simultaneously displaying faith and works. According to Jesus, the most important commandment is "love your neighbor as yourself". Jesus then went on to explain that for anyone who loved their neighbors as they did themselves, keeping the other nine commandments would not be difficult.

The teachings of Jesus can frequently lead one to ask him or herself if Christ is present in many churches that profess His name. When discussing this topic, the portion of scripture that comes to mind is when Christ said "that on the Judgment Day many would come to Him and say, Lord I have served you all my life, and he would reply to them to get away from me for I never knew you." This statement by our lord Jesus is profound because He is saying that many people that hold themselves out to be Christians would not be entering Heaven. It is not my place to judge anyone and as the Lord has so elegantly stated, "Judge not and you would not be judged."

Today, Father's day – June 18th 2017 – I began my day by watching the preaching of Pastor Jessie Duplantis of Jessie Duplantis Ministries and Dr. Charles Stanley of In Touch ministries . Both had very similar sermons; the sermons of Dr. Jessie Duplantis were primarily on the issue of kindness and going a step further. To this, he used the story of Rebecca and the circumstances leading to her being picked to be the wife of Isaac, the son of Abraham.

Dr. Stanley's sermon was primarily on the rule of sowing or the rule of harvest. The rule of harvest is that you reap more than what you sow. The big question here is what happens to people that reap what they did not sow? This can either be a good or a bad non-harvest. I say non-harvest because in some instances, people may reap what they did not sow. The question now becomes when and how would such peoples' true harvest be realized?

CHAPTER 14

THE PSYCHOLOGY OF FALSE ALLEGATIONS

What effects do false allegations have on one's psyche when one knows that the allegations are false but lots of the general public believe those allegations to be true? This situation is the ultimate test of strong will or will power. It's what defines – or one could say – reveals one's true character and inner strength. It's my belief that the truth will eventually be revealed. As it is said in Bible, there is no way – short of putting out a light – to prevent it from shining in the darkness. It may sound childlike or naive, but it's also my belief that truth cannot be hidden indefinitely. The truth can only be hidden for long periods of time when the righteous individual forsakes pursuing the truth or for whatever reason is convinced that the truth is not worth finding.

How does this scenario relate to my experiences over the last four and a half years? The New York Attorney General's Office – in its attempt to build a case against me – reported that between the period of January 2009 and September 30, 2011, I submitted vouchers totaling $747,139.00. However, what the New York State Attorney General's Office intentionally failed to report is that those very vouchers were for the years 2006, 2007, 2008, 2009, 2010, and 2011. The story was worded to give the impression that the work performed was for the period of January 2009 through September 30, 2011. The Attorney General's Office had access to all of my submitted vouchers. Therefore, there is no reason to believe that a mistake was made. It was a deliberate attempt to ruin my reputation and degrade my character, all based on false information and allegations.

Capitalism, although it can be a very good system, is not without deep and serious flaws. The flaw here is that individuals are attempting to make themselves, or build their professional reputations by almost any means necessary.

Today, June 29, 2017: Court Incident

Today, a somewhat unusual occurrence happened in court. While in the midst of an inquiry and deliberation, the courtroom microphone that was located closest to me and my client accidentally fell on the courtroom floor. While outside the courtroom but still within the courthouse, the court officer inquired of myself and my client if either of us happened to have kicked or somehow made contact with the microphone – hence causing it to fall. Both my client and myself replied that we had no physical contact with the microphone. After asking me a second time whether I made any physical contact with the device before it fell, my client replied saying or implying, "Why are you asking my attorney such a question? He is a lawyer".

After my client made this remark, both the court officers – one who happened to be an African American female – laughed emphatically. Whatever motivation I suspected they had for having reacted in such a manner was purely speculative but perhaps, it had to do with the stereotypes about lawyers that the general public often subscribes to. Or perhaps their response had something to do with my previous legal encounter. Also, worth noting is that the other individual involved in that emphatic laugh is herself an attorney, who happens to be Caucasian. Of course, this brings to mind my current pending lawsuit against the defendants, New York State, and Broome County. Three of the seventeen counts in my pending lawsuit are slander, libel, and defamation of character.

Now I am not in any position to say with any level of certainty why my client's remark of 'why are you asking him this question? He is a lawyer!' was met with such reaction. It's my opinion that my three counts of libel, slander, and defamation of character are very well founded.

About six months ago, I had another similar situation in another courthouse. This time, it was with the assistant county prosecutor who told me that I got away because the Attorney General's Office presented a "weak" case. To me, implying that I was guilty, but the Attorney General's Office was ineffective in presenting their case. She then went on to state that according to what's on the internet, I billed $747,000.00. According to that assistant county prosecutor, I billed $350,000.00 per year for two years. She then went on to say that no one would get away with such a thing in her county.

Based on my experience and on comments and reactions like those just mentioned, I am left with no choice but to restate my belief that America's jails and prisons are filled with scores of innocent people. It's also very unfortunate that the vast majority of those innocent people in America's jails and prisons are minorities and disproportionately African Americans. For all of the above reasons, I am unable to support the death penalty. I may even go one step further and say that for lots of individuals, the death penalty can rightfully be described as cruel and unusual punishment.

CHAPTER 15

THE AUDACITY OF HOPE

As was previously mentioned in this book, one of the most difficult challenges to face and was primarily induced in the event of October 11, 2012 is the resulting financial challenges that are heaped on me. Throughout the almost five-year ordeal (October 2012 to today, July 9th, 2017), both of my children are and have been attending university. It is particularly challenging when undergoing financial hardship with college or university children because there is always an expense to be incurred or an event to partake in. Such expenses can be foreseen or unforeseen. However, one of the most striking realizations is that one's hopes and dreams for their children is never diminished during tough times. Today - July 9, 2017 – as I am faced with many challenges, I can foresee my oldest son pursuing higher education and receiving both his medical and law degree. I can also see my younger son pursuing higher education and earning both his law degree and his Master of Business Administration degree. It is also my realization that difficult times do not destroy one's dreams, but strengthens them.

Today, my children's dreams and accomplishments have become more important than my own. Although, in all honesty, I must say that nowhere in my wildest dreams did I envision the experience that I went through from 2012 to today. No one could've dreamed of such experiences. The question I very frequently asked myself is: how can I use my lifelong experiences to benefit others? This question has not yet been fully answered, but I stand very confident that sometime within the very near future, it would be clearly and precisely answered. When the discussion using my lifelong experience to be of help to others, I am not just referring to individuals in the United States. It's my belief that such experiences can be applied and be of assistance beyond national and international borders.

One of the outcomes of such experiences is the ability to tailor one's goals and aspirations to a more practical, realistic, and achievable level. The biggest mistake that can be made after such an experience is the overgeneralization of people or individuals and attachment of negative labels to them. There could also be a tendency of viewing individuals as being more bad than good. This is something that I frequently struggle with. However, whenever experiencing such thoughts, one must remember that the Maker of the Universe, the one that had no sin but suffered and was crucified for our salvation had far worse experiences than we can and will ever undergo. We should also remember that all mankind has sinned and fallen short of the glory of God, but Jesus – our Savior – knew no sin. The question now becomes if Jesus – the Son of man –knew no sin and was convicted and crucified in man's court of law, why should we expect to not have our difficult encounters in this imperfect world? Jesus has promised us that He would never leave us nor forsake us. However, He never promised us a life free of troubles, deception, and wrongful allegations. Also of tremendous importance is that Jesus was opposed and condemned by the religious men of His day.

One of the most meaningful consequences of difficult times is not that one's hopes and dreams never die, but it is the degree in which one's hope and determination are strengthened. In short, hard or difficult times can birth new and realistic undertakings.

CHAPTER 16

STANDING AT THE CROSSROADS

Today – July 18, 2017 – at about 9:30 pm, I received a telephone call from my youngest son thanking us for the great job that we did for him. Thanking us – my wife and I – for affording him such great opportunities, stating how proud he is of his parents, both immigrants, for our major accomplishments in the United States of America. From my son's point of view, he is of the belief that he could have accomplished much more at his age had he listened to me when he was younger. According to him, everything that was said to him in his earlier life was now making lots of sense, and his only regret was that he didn't listen more attentively when he was younger at the age of fourteen. He stated that he is of the belief that had he paid more attention to the things he was taught and told by his parents earlier in life, he would have now been attending an Ivy League university.

From my point of view, my son has accomplished a lot, and there is nothing more that could be expected of him. He is now a senior at a very well-respected university. He is 20 years of age is on the Dean's List, and will be a commissioned military officer at the age of twenty-one. He had the opportunity to attend West Point Academy but passed up the opportunity because at the time he was going into his junior year of university and was a junior in the Reserve Officer Training Corps (ROTC) and did not want to repeat a freshman year at West Point Academy. Had he attended West Point Academy, he would've been starting all over as a freshman. So, he decided against it. Tonight, after my conversation with my youngest son, it dawned on me that the very same scenario that currently existed between me and my son was very similar to my contemporary relationship with my father. It's my opinion that I could have accomplished much more in my life, but my father totally disagrees. According to my father, I have excelled with the cards that were dealt to me. My father, who is currently 100 years of age, is of the opinion that I have excelled in the game of life, and that I have overachieved. I am not of that opinion.

While it is true that I am a first-generation immigrant, being born in the Caribbean and immigrated to the U.S. at the age of twenty, it's my belief that I could have accomplished more than I actually did. Both my son and my father strongly disagree with that point of view.

Shortly after my arrival in the U.S, I enlisted in the military. At the age of twenty-four, I completed my first tour of active military duty and then embarked on my college career while serving in the U.S Army Reserve, the Texas Army National Guard, and the New York Army National Guard. I earned an associate's degree, a bachelor's degree, a master's degree, a law degree, and to date have completed all requirements, except my dissertation, for my (PhD) doctorate degree. This I hope to complete in the very near future.

Unlike my son that will earn his military commission at the age of twenty-one, I earned my military commission at the age of twenty-six. My hope is that my son – after receiving his military commission and completing his Officer's Basic Course – would pursue a joint (JD) law degree and Masters of Business Administration. That is my immediate hope and wish for him.

The Cross Road

I named this chapter "Standing at the Crossroads" because I really feel that I am at a cross-road in my life. As I am currently writing this chapter in my second book entitled *Road to Recovery*, I am truly at a crossroad. In my pending lawsuit against New York State and the County of Broome, I stand eagerly awaiting a judge's ruling that I believe has the capacity to change or alter my life, both currently – the immediate future and the very distant future. It's also my belief that the judge's ruling can have very far-reaching consequences affecting the future generations of my family. I have submitted the appropriate documents and have asked for a default judgment against the defendants, New York State, and the County of Broome. Should my motion be granted, this will be a significant game changer.

Although tonight I reminded my son that he should always work hard and not take any shortcuts in life, it must be stated and remembered that it was my work ethic that led both New York State and the County of Broome to bring false allegations of cheating and fraud against me. How disappointing is it that so many people still don't realize that most immigrants do not immigrate to the United States to party, drive fancy cars, and wear the most expensive clothes. I am sure that many immigrants have succumbed to that lifestyle and way of thinking, but I am not one of them and probably never will be.

Please do not be of the opinion that I am condemning America's way of life because that is the last thing I intend to do. In every society there is good and there is bad. One's decision should be to pick the path most comfortable to him or her. I have never been attracted to glitz and glamour, and in most probability, the chances are that I never will be. Glitz and glamour just does not appeal to me. So that part of America, I have soundly rejected. I can recall as a young enlisted soldier in the U.S Army spending many nights at the non- commissioned officers' club on the military base. I can also recall many of my new acquaintances-- young soldiers-- that I have met on base and particularly at the non-commissioned officers' club trying to persuade me to upgrade my wardrobe. The truth of the matter is that I was much more interested in upgrading my education than I was my wardrobe. I was content not being the best dressed man at the club, but was not content with not being the most educated man in the club. The end result was that I invested heavily into my educational savings plan and not so much on my wardrobe.

CHAPTER 17

MY WORK ETHIC AND DRIVE FOR HIGHER EDUCATION

My work ethic and drive for higher education are the traits and habits I received from my father. I cannot talk very much about my mother because I never knew her. She died in a house fire when I was two years of age. After initially escaping the house once it caught fire, she ultimately returned to the house to rescue us. We were rescued from the fire, but she never escaped.

My father would regularly use my mother's death as a means of motivating us. He would frequently say to me that my mother is already dead, and he is the only one of our parents that's left, so should he die we would have no one. He would frequently say that whenever he wanted us to do well or to do better in school. We were always and very regularly encouraged to do well or excel in school because according to my father, "education is our only hope." All four of our grandparents - both maternal and paternal – were deceased.

THE ROAD TO RECOVERY

Growing up in the Caribbean, I was a good athlete. I participated in or played three different sports: soccer, cricket, and track and field. I liked all three sports equally, but was never encouraged by my father to become a serious athlete. In fact, he would frequently discourage me from pursuing an athletic career. To him, there was no future in pursuing a career in athletics because it was too risky. According to my father, all it would take to end my athletic career is a broken leg. To him, that was not good enough; education was the only sure thing. He succeeded in convincing me, and this led to me pursuing a career in academics. I had the opportunity of serving as an adjunct professor for three years-- a job that I really loved and enjoyed. That is one of the reasons why after so many years, I have not given up or forsaken my PhD in Economics. It's my belief that I would once again be able to teach both Law and Economics at the college or university Level. The non-completion of my PhD dissertation was primarily due to my very busy legal practice. The real irony of this story is that I was accused of cheating, something that I would never do.

My advice to my children is to always work hard, but please be diversified. Too much of one thing is good for nothing and not only that, but if their luck is anything like mine, they may be accused of also cheating. Another piece of advice I regularly received from my father is: do not waste your time (gossiping) talking about people. Let people talk about you but before you waste valuable time gossiping about people, it would be more productive to find yourself a second job. That would afford you the opportunity to live off the income generated from one job, while you invest the income earned from your second job".

My father was a single parent long before it was acceptable to be a single parent. He raised all of his children and to this day has never remarried. Like my father, I cannot see myself remarrying under about any circumstance. Most shocking to me is the way in which my father, myself, and my son are so very similar. Maybe it is true that the apple does not fall far from the tree. However, one big difference between my father and I is that I encouraged my son to participate in organized sports much more than my father encouraged me. Subconsciously, that could be because in the United States there is a strong probability that one can earn a comfortable income and secure a comfortable standard of living and way of life by becoming a professional athlete. This factor was virtually non-existent when I was a child growing up in the Caribbean. It can also be that in the Caribbean having a profession such as a doctor or lawyer is much more prestigious than being an athlete. Being an athlete in the Caribbean during the time of my youth was not very glamorous or attractive of an endeavor. This I believe has changed or is rapidly changing.

CHAPTER 18

WORK LOAD/ WORK SCHEDULE PRIOR TO OCTOBER 12, 2012 AND AFTER OCTOBER 12, 2017

One of the most striking differences prior to October 12, 2012 and post October 12, 2012 is my workload or work-schedule. Prior to October 12, 2012, I had an average of six (6) court appearances daily. On some days, it could be as much as ten or more court appearances. Alternatively, on the low end, on some days my court appearances could be as few as one or two. However, my practice was steady and consistent. During those heavy and consistent times, my daily schedule was as follows. I would wake up at about 3:00 AM – 4:00 AM to get ready for trial. Also, during those prosperous times, I had an average of five (5) trials per week. This is because I had routinely and consistently worked in three counties. The counties where I routinely worked prior to October 12, 2012 are Broome County, where I have resided for a number of years, Tioga County – an adjoining county to Broome

County, and Delaware County – another adjoining county to Broome County. Today, the county where I work most often is Tioga County. My appearances in both the Broome County and the Delaware County courtrooms and courthouses have significantly diminished. To continue with my routine schedule prior to October 11, 2012, I wake up around 3:00 AM to 4:00 AM daily. I would prepare for my daily court trials from my home office. This home office is where I initially launched my private practice. Prior to opening my downtown office, I worked exclusively from my home office. However, I fell in love with my home office and decided to keep it. It came in very handy, and, after all, it was my first office. After completion of my daily routine trial preparation, I would begin preparation either to go directly to court or, in the event that my court appearances or trials were later in the day, I would proceed to my office. On average, I would depart from my office between 5:00 and 6:00 PM daily. Of course, there are occasional exceptions to my schedule. After arriving at my home after 6:00 PM, I would have supper then relax for approximately thirty minutes to one hour. Then I would go to the jail - most often in Broome County but occasionally in Tioga County Jail or Delaware County Jail.

Because of my rigorous schedule and the numerous hours of work daily I routinely expounded into my practice, being accused of any type of professional dishonesty was a huge shock and surprise to me.

The Bottom Line of a Significantly Reduced Work Schedule

January 4, 2016, my first day back to work, and in my office was very similar to my very first day of private legal practice. Everything was very slow. A slowness that I had grown unaccustomed to.

CHAPTER 19

THE GREATEST POINT IN A LIFE

It is widely believed that the greatest point in a person's life is when he or she is at the bottom of their career, economic standing or financially. This is the point in one's life when a friend is usually very hard to find. It is also the point in one's life when true friends would be made, or it would reveal who your friends are and in many instances, truly reveal if one ever had any friends. This point in one's life reveals their true character.

There is, however, a great and honorable characteristic to being at the lowest point in one's life; that is for many people the place and time when most of their best, most rewarding, and long lasting decisions are made. That is the point in one's life where all decisions or promises made would most likely be kept. It is, in fact, the greatest point in one's life. Another great characteristic about being at a low point in life is that one usually has a clear view to the very top and what's necessary to get there. There is no place else to go but up. There is an old saying that says "It is much harder to fail than it is to succeed." Attempting or trying to keep a man down requires extraordinarily hard work. The end result is usually that the individual with the intent of limiting one's success would only succeed in limiting his or her own success. When I was approximately ten years of age, my father told me that you can never keep a good man down. Today, my experience seems to hint that he was very correct. Today, in this small and interdependent and interconnected world, opportunities can emerge from anywhere and at any time. This makes it very scary to even entertain the thought of limiting one's success, or in the short term, trying to keep someone down.

Also, very fascinating, is that the same principles apply to most or many countries. In today's world, because there is no longer any dominant superpower, it is very difficult to successfully embargo any particular country. Today, we have about three or four countries desperately fighting for world economic dominance. To some individuals, this may be seen as a good thing and to others it may be seen as a bad thing. The end result is that no one country can dictate the future of another. There is another old saying, which is widely believed by many to be true, and that is the notion that "Countries behave like their citizens." In short, in the aggregate, a country would behave in the same way or manner as its citizens.

International economics is a topic that is very near and dear to my heart; in that vein, let's discuss an economic embargo placed by one country against another. In today's world climate, it is almost impossible for one country to be able to successfully place an economic embargo against another. The reason being that there are other countries that produce similar goods and services that are in demand in the economic embargoed nation. The embargoed nation can or would usually find a way or devise a plan to get the needed goods into the embargoed market. This is one reason why OPEC was not very reliable and, in some instances, ineffective. The acronym OPEC stands for Oil Producing and Exporting Countries. OPEC was a cartel whose purpose was to restrict oil prices or to keep the price of oil competitive in the world's market. This goal was accomplished primarily by restricting the production and exports of crude oil.

It should be noted that is a form of collusion or price fixing and is illegal on its face in the United States. Thus, OPEC was never able to make any of its price fixing, or restriction of oil production agreements on U.S soil or in any U.S territories. It is simply an illegal agreement under U.S law and under the laws of all fifty states.

The 1950's US Embargo

In the 1950's, shortly after the Bay of Pigs era, the U.S placed economic embargo on the Caribbean island nation of Cuba. Except for humanitarian needs and assistance, virtually all exports and trade between the U.S and Cuba were legally prohibited. It is a long and widely held belief that the Cuban economy suffered in many ways because of the U.S embargo. There were also lots of benefits enjoyed by the Castro regime because of the U.S actions against Cuba. First and most important, the U.S was widely seen by many throughout the world as a big "bully" attempting to impose its will on a smaller, and as the U.S sees it, a vulnerable nation. However, it is also believed by many that the U.S actions against Cuba were largely responsible for "fostering togetherness and national pride" among the Cuban people. One can also report that despite the U.S embargo and sanctions against Cuba, there were many countries that disregarded the U.S embargo and conducted regular business with the island nation of Cuba. Today, Cuba is widely believed to be one of the best nations in the Caribbean despite its pockets of poverty. It has a very rich culture, and its natural resources and beauty were never fully exploited. Cuba today is a nature lover's paradise. It has very little pollution, and it is one of the few places in the world where nature is somewhat fully intact and well maintained. It also has very blue sea water and very scenic coral reefs that are somewhat untouched by man's massive pollution machine. To many individuals, the aforementioned facts about the Caribbean island nation were well worth the U.S embargo. The question now becomes, should relations between Cuba and the United States become normalized? Would Cuba be able to maintain or hold on to its natural beauty? How would it reduce man made pollution? The notion of this U.S and Cuban story is that there is cost and benefits to everything, even an economic embargo. This brings to mind a conversation I had with a Bahamian citizen many years ago. She was a Bahamian school teacher that applied for and received a leave of absence in order to study in the U.S. She mentioned some words that I may never forget. She said, "Americans visit the Bahamas for vacation, and Bahamians go to Cuba to spend their vacations." Is that a coincidence, or a dramatic irony? It's left up to the readers to decide. Or better yet, the readers would decide.

CHAPTER 20

THE POWER OF THE SUPERNATURAL

There are three times in my life when I sincerely believed that I had an other- than- natural experience, or I should say a supernatural experience. Please allow me the pleasure of addressing those experiences in chronological order.

My first supernatural experience occurred in approximately between the year 1999 and 2000. At that time my wife and I, with our two young children were residing in Binghamton, New York and were renting a two- bedroom, second floor apartment. It's my recollection that I went to bed that night in a routine manner. There was nothing special or extraordinary going on or taking place that night. It is my belief that I went to bed at approximately 10:30 pm that night. I, then, fell asleep. Sometime during the night while fully asleep, I experienced myself or saw myself, in soul or spirit, depart from my body, and myself, or my soul or my spirit began ascending upward in the sky. During my ascent I looked down and saw my body lying on the bed, but I was not in my body. That was the best experience I ever had. It was like euphoria. It was euphoric. Up until that moment, I never had anything or any experience so comforting in my entire life. During my ascent, I was not alone. There was someone else present with me. Up to this day, I can vividly remember the words spoken to me by that unknown man that was present during my departure from my physical body. The masculine voice of the man whose face I did not see said "As wonderful as this experience is for you, it could have been even better." Up to today, I am unable to understand what this strange man, whose face I did not see, meant when he said to me "as wonderful as this experience is for you, it could have been even better". I keep asking myself, is there something I am supposed to do that I have not done? Are There some unrepented sins, or sin in my life? Am I supposed to get more involved in organizations of faith? Am I supposed to get involved in helping the poor? Am I not paying my tithes to the Church? Or am I not making the appropriate offerings? What is it that I have done and should not have done? Or what is it that I am supposed to do that I have not done?

It's my hope that with time, the mystery underlying this statement from a man whose face I have not seen would reveal itself to me. That was such a great experience, that it can't be compared to any other experience I had in this world. I never wanted that experience to end, but I eventually re-entered my body.

Shortly after that experience, I was of the belief that my death was near, or simply put, that I would not have a very long time left on this Earth so I purchased life insurance for the protection of my family should I soon thereafter depart from this world or Universe.

My second super-natural experience occurred within one year of my first supernatural experience. It occurred in the very same two-bedroom second floor apartment where my first supernatural experience had occurred. I can vividly remember and recall when I made a committed decision to study the Bible, and to read the entire Bible from the first book of Genesis to the last book of Revelation. There are sixty-six books in the Bible. The Book of Genesis being the first, and the Book of Revelation being the last.

That night when I made the decision to study in depth the entire bible, it's my recollection that I started with the Book of Matthew, in the New Testament. After I read the first two chapters in the Book of Matthew, I stopped reading the Bible for that night and placed a mark at the point where I stopped reading. I was not ready or expecting what occurred shortly thereafter. A complete and total peace came over me. It was a complete inner peace. The type of peace that is not of this world. I can write about that inner peace, but it's my belief that in order to fully understand it, one must themselves experience it. It is that type of peace that cannot be obtained from this world. It's my belief and opinion, that this world is not capable of giving anyone such peace, nor is the world capable of taking such peace away from anyone that experiences it. It is a complete inner experience; there was a man or a male spirit present in that apartment that night. I felt the presence of that man, but I did not see his face. But I am certain that a male or a male spirit was present with me in my second floor, two- bedroom apartment that night. But once again I did not see his face.

<u>My third supernatural experience</u> occurred in a Broome County courtroom on or about August 14, 2014. I appeared in court to hear the false allegations made against me by the State of New York and to a certain extent, the County of Broome. This was the beginning of my political trial that ended in all charges against me being dismissed. As the charges and allegations against me were being read, a total and complete peace came all over me. The allegations may have been serious but very few people would believe me if I told them how at peace I felt. It was as if nothing serious was happening, and I was not being accused of anything. Even I myself was surprised and amazed with how at ease and at peace I was in the courtroom on that day.

CHAPTER 21

THE RACIAL INCIDENCES OF CHARLOTTESVILLE ON 12TH AUGUST, 2017

On August 12th, 2017, there was a "Unite the Right" rally that was composed of numerous ultra- right groups from all over the United States. Some of the groups involved in that rally were the Ku Klux Klan (KKK), the Neo-nazi party, and several other white supremacist groups, which included Vanguard of America. The end result of that rally was three fatalities and at least nineteen other people injured. Of the three people killed, one was a thirty- two- year old female and two Virginia State Police officers, both in their forties .

Lots of people seem to be amazed by the events that unfolded yesterday in Charlottesville, Virginia, but for some strange and unknown reason I was not one bit surprised. It is also my belief that we can expect many more of such rallies in many other states and locations throughout the Unites States.

It is unsure as to the role played by race and economic standing in society that can lead large amounts of people to have that much hate and resentment toward their fellow men.

CHAPTER 22

CAPITALISM AND ITS PITFALLS AND UNCERTAINTIES

Capitalism, although hailed by many as the best system to grace this Earth, is fraught with pitfalls and uncertainties. It is well understood that in a Capitalist system a man or woman can lose everything he or she owns if struck with an illness, a divorce, or for any other unforeseen or unanticipated incident or activity. However, it is my belief that it has not been thought of by many that in a Capitalist system, an individual can go bankrupt and lose all of their lives accumulations, or lives material possessions by false allegations and charges made and brought against them. One might be tempted to say that in a Capitalist society, as far as worldly possessions go "easy come easy go". But for the vast majority of the people residing in Capitalist societies throughout this world, nothing comes easy, especially material or earthly possessions. On the contrary, possessions that was or is earned with blood, sweat and tears, could dissipate in the blink of an eye. There lies the difference between a Marxist, Socialist or centrally planned and administered economy in which worldly possessions are almost impossible to accumulate, but whatever one is able to gather or accumulate during ones working life is almost impossible to lose. For example, in most centrally planned societies, citizens and adults have government paid for, or government sponsored educational system, and health systems, as a result citizens have little fear of losing all of their material possessions due to an unforeseen illness. Additionally, in socialist, Marxist or other centrally planned economies, students as a rule do not graduate from college with huge educational debts. In short, there exists no perfect political or economic system; a good political economic system is one that maximizes social benefits for the greatest amount of its citizens. Perfection is only a dream, and such wishful thinking that can only exist in heaven.

However, it is my belief that Capitalism will never die, because as the old saying goes "Hope springs eternal". In most free market societies, the poor and less economically endowed individuals, almost always believe that a chance exists for going from rags to riches. Additionally, in many instances after people have lost their economic fortune, there is always a hope of regaining and surpassing their lost fortunes. It is also a true statement that most millionaires were bankrupt at least once or twice in their lifetime. There is also an old saying that "it is easier to achieve success, once one had experienced success". Getting back on top is easier once one was already on top as opposed to someone who has never been on top or has never experienced success.

With all the negative side effects of capitalism and capitalist societies, if given the free choice to pick between socialism, Marxism and capitalism, it is my belief that a majority of the world's seven or eight (7-8) billion people would choose or prefer to reside in a Capitalist society. There is an old saying that "socialism or communism will never succeed in the United States of America, because a vast majority of the less economically successful Americans view themselves as failed capitalists merely awaiting their opportunities for success". This belief lends credence to the thought or saying that "hope springs eternal".

CHAPTER 23

MY LAWSUIT AGAINST NEW YORK STATE AND THE COUNTY OF BROOME

On or about the 8th of May 2017, I filed a claim/lawsuit against both Broome County and the State of New York. This claim/lawsuit was filed in the New York State Court of Claims in Albany, New York. The suit contained, outlined, and mentioned seventeen counts of wrongdoing against me by the State of New York and by the County of Broome. On or about the 30th of May 2017, both the State of New York and the County of Broome were officially served with the claim/lawsuit.

About three weeks thereafter, the County of Broome was served with a claim/lawsuit; the County of Broome made a motion in the Court of Claims asking the Court to dismiss the lawsuit against them because the Court of Claims has jurisdiction only over the state of New York, but lacks jurisdiction over Broome County and its agencies. I vigorously argued against dismissing the claim/suit against Broome County, but failed in my argument to keep the County of Broome as a defendant in this matter. My arguments to deny the County's motion were primarily predicated on the fact that the County was a major player in the failed prosecution, and because the county was a major player in all the earlier legal events, they reaped the benefit and costs of the initial trial and, therefore, should be held accountable for their actions. This principle is based on the common law notion of pendent jurisdiction. According to the common law principle, pendent jurisdiction is proper whenever all ensuing actions arise, or has arisen, from the same facts or circumstances. This, in my estimation, is a perfect case to utilize the principle of pendent jurisdiction. The State of New York and the County of Broome were equally responsible for prior legal matters, and should therefore be responsible for the damages caused by their wrongful actions.

Before going any further, it is important to explain the duties and responsibilities of the New York State Court of Claims. The primary function of the New York State Court of Claims is to compensate individuals that were harmed by the State of New York. Its primary function is to award monetary compensation for wrongs committed against individuals and, or privately-owned property. The Court of Claims is a court of limited jurisdiction and has jurisdiction over claims against the State of New York and a limited number of other entities established by statute (NY Constitution, Article VI Court of Claims Act Section

9). It has exclusive jurisdiction over actions for financial money damages against the state that are based on wrongful state action or inaction.

Utilizing that rationale, the court dismissed all claims against Broome County, stating that "the Court of Claims has no jurisdiction over the county or its employees including the District Attorney".

It should be noted that from the date of filing the claim/complaint against Broome County up to the issuance of the decision and order dismissing all counts in the claim/petition against Broome County, there were no court appearances. All decisions were made on submission only, meaning that neither party nor parties were scheduled to make any court appearances, and no court appearance was made by either side or party.

Motion for Default Judgment and the First Court Appearance

Today, October 4, 2018, I'm awaiting the court's decision and my motion for default judgment made against New York State for failure to answer a duly filed and duly served claim/petition. On May 30, 2017, the New York State Attorney General's Office was served with the claim/petition seeking damages under the seventeen count claim/petition. I am using the words "claim/petition" because this matter was filed with the New York State Court of Claims. In the Court of Claims, the word claimant is used as being synonymous with plaintiff or petitioner.

Pursuant to the law governing the Court of Claims, "The Court of Claims Act", a claim is properly filed when a claimant prepares a claim, files said claim with the Court of Claims in Albany New York, and finally serves a copy of the claim that is filed and stamped by the Court of Claims on the respondent. A claim can either be filed by personal service upon the defendant or by certified mail with return receipt. There is one additional step that must occur prior to the claim being docketed, that is, either an affidavit of service upon the respondent must be returned to the Court of Claims or a stamped copy of the first page of the claim with a stamp and date received by the Attorney General Office, must be returned to the court of claims within two weeks of service upon the New York State Attorney General's office. Only after those four steps were properly executed is a lawful claim filed with the Court of Claims.

Upon serving a copy of the claim to the respondent, the Attorney General Office, they have forty days to respond to the claim. However, in some instances, the law allows a certain number of days for mailing.

After forty-seven days of service upon the Attorney General's Office, there was no answer/response form the said office to the claim. The Attorney General's Office defense was that they had previously responded to a courtesy copy of the claim that was given to them prior to the filing with the Court of Claims Office in Albany, New York. The major problem here is that no claim is properly filed until or unless filed with the Court of Claims office in Albany. Hence, utilizing that rationale, a claim cannot be properly served unless it is properly filed with the Court of Claims office in Albany, New York. Thus, based on my years of legal education and years of legal practice, a courtesy copy of the claim that was given to the Attorney General's Office was premature and doesn't constitute proper service. However, the court disagreed with my reasoning and held that "a claim does not have to be filed with the Court of Claims Office in Albany, New York before it can be served upon the New York State Attorney General's Office.

The Attorney General's Office second defense for the motion to default judgment is that there was no change in contents and or allegations between the courtesy copy of the claim that was given to them prior to the official filing in Albany, and the claim that was properly served on them; therefore, service upon them after filing in Albany was not necessary. The Attorney General's second defense is also without merit because the official or properly filed claim/petition has nothing to do with the content of the claim, but instead whether the proper process was followed. Based on my legal education and experience, both of the Attorney General's arguments are without merit. It is my opinion, based on my legal education and many years of legal experience that the judge is left with no choice but to render a decision favorable to me. However, the court ruled that the Court of Claims is unlike any other court and the strict pleading rules applied in City Courts, County Courts and State Supreme Court does not apply in the Court of Claims.

The motion for default judgment was heard on submission only on September 13, 2017 at 09:00 AM, on submission only is a legal term that means "no appearances necessary." Neither the claimant/petitioner nor the defendant/respondent is required to be present in court. The ruling would be based on all of the submissions/paperwork that both parties submitted to the court concerning this matter.

A motion to default judgment can be dispositive to a case. This means that should the judge rule in the claimant's favor, the case is basically over. The Court has the option of either granting the damages requested in the claim, or the court can hold an inquest hearing to determine damages. An inquest hearing is one based solely on facts to determine the amount of damages warranted. However, an inquest hearing is not mandatory, since the court is free to grant the damages requested in the petition.

CHAPTER 24

THE PSYCHOLOGY OF POVERTY

Unlike what is currently believed by many, it is my belief that poverty starts in one's mind. It is not racism that creates poverty but the way that one thinks. This chapter may seem to be a diversion from the title of the book, *The Road to Recovery*, but it should not be because one's ability to recover from difficulties, including financial difficulties, depends, to a large degree, on their thinking process. In short, one's financial standing and their standard in life is more mental than physical. Some may argue that how about individuals that have inherited fortunes from their predecessors? Does that concept apply to them? How an individual handles their inherited wealth is also a feature of their thinking process. It is written in the Bible that "a fool and his money will soon depart." This statement is absolutely correct. However, in the vast majority of instances, the fool will not accumulate any money.

Today – October 23, 2017 – I went to the home of a tenant who is in the process of eviction for non-payment of rent. To my surprise, that tenant's apartment is fully decorated for the upcoming Halloween festivities. I asked myself, wouldn't that money be better spent paying the monthly rent? Let's assume that this tenant is evicted for non-payment of rent. The tenant will now become homeless. The ultimate question becomes, where and how would homeless individuals celebrate Halloween? Although, I do understand that everyone needs some relief and an outlet to be away from the sadness of daily life, we must make decisions that would improve our economic standing in the long and very long run and learn to forgo instant gratification. We all must learn how to make sacrifices for the betterment of ourselves in the long run and in the very long run. The long run could be a period of about one to five years and the "very long run" is for periods in excess of five years.

As stated on many occasions in this book, had God not given me the foresight to invest in real estate during my prosperous years, how would I have survived today? I am not in any way doing one eight (1/8) as well as I should've been doing, but it would've been much worse had I not made some long- term investments over the years. I have lost a lot of income and investments over the last five years, but I am very thankful for whatever I am left with.

Racism, although it's a major contributing factor to the poverty and in some cases hopelessness of many individuals, is in and of itself not enough to be the main or only cause of poverty. Racism increases the difficulty of some individuals to achieve success, while acting as a catalyst for pushing others to succeed. In short, for some individuals, racism is analogous to a headwind, delaying and pushing back against their success. For others, it's like a tailwind pushing them towards success.

After reading this paragraph, I am somewhat certain that most readers will be surprised that the tenant whose apartment I went to this morning were neither African Americans nor Latinos. They are in fact white tenants.

Illogical thinking is present in every race. However, the difference is that some races, due to societal makeup, are less predisposed to society's negative stigma.

CHAPTER 25

INSTITUTIONAL RACISM – THE AMERICA WAY

As I prepare for my Fifth (5th) Thanksgiving Day and my fifth Christmas since my 2012 ordeal, I keep asking myself: what would the U.S be without institutional racism? Would it have been a better country without it? Prior to October 12, 2012, I probably had the busiest law office in the city of Binghamton and maybe in the entirety of Broome County. But since then, it has been a constant struggle. Does institutionalized racism mean that wealth and prosperity should be limited to certain individuals? There are so many side effects to institutional racism; however, I believe that the most significant of those effects is on children. Forcing children of negatively affected families to endure needless struggle and having to make do with less of almost everything. The overall effect of institutional racism on young children is substantial, and in many cases, indelible.

<u>Chief Justice, New York State Appellate Division – 3rd Judicial Department and Abuse of Power</u>

Today, the 21st of November 2017, over two years since I was victorious in a wrongful and political trial against me, I received astonishing news. In January, 2016, when I reopened my law office on a full-time basis, I continuously received legal assignments from Tioga County, a small county adjacent to Broome County. However, it eventually came to my attention that my last assignment from Tioga County Court was in August, 2017. After a brief thought about this situation, I called the Tioga County Family Court to inquire whether my name was currently on the list of attorneys willing to accept assignments in the Tioga County Court System. After a brief conversation with the court clerk, I was referred to the judge's secretary who informed me that the court was informed by the administrative office of the third judicial department that I should be allowed to complete all my existing assigned cases, but no new cases should be assigned to me. Upon being informed of such, I was very dismayed. It's been two years since this matter was tried in a court of law, and all of the members of the jury reached a unanimous conclusion that no wrongdoing was committed by me.

CHAPTER 26

CHRISTMAS 2017 VACATION IN TORONTO, CANADA

Today, December 27, 2017, I visited my in-laws in Toronto Canada, I made a trip to Buffalo, New York with my youngest son. His car broke down, he blew his engine, and the car was sold to an auction company to be sold to a vehicle auction, within the upcoming weeks or within the next vehicle auction.

Both of my sons are now graduating from college, the oldest with a Bachelor's degree in Biomedical Engineering and Chemistry. His plan is to attend medical school. However, I am actively trying to persuade him to attend both medical school and law school. I am doing so because I am convinced that he has the mental and intellectual aptitude to become both a medical doctor and a lawyer. My youngest son will be having two graduation ceremonies in May of 2018. One is for his Bachelor's degree in Business Administration, with a concentration in Finance and Logistics, and a military graduation to become an officer in the U.S Army. He will be completing his

Reserve Officer's Training Corps (ROTC) program, which leads to him becoming a commissioned officer in the U.S. Army.

While driving with my son to Buffalo, New York from Toronto Canada, it again dawned on me that throughout both of my children's educational careers, I've been undergoing wrongful financial hardship brought upon me by individuals seeking to make a name for themselves at any and all cost. Additionally, it is my belief that my youngest son has the intellect and mental aptitude to become a great attorney. Hence, I'm also trying to convince him to attend law school.

However, looking back at the last five years, beginning from October 11, 2012 to the present, it also dawned on me that I have a great deal to be thankful for. Despite the financial hardship heaped upon me and my family, my sons have performed exceptionally well in their educational endeavors. Could it be that hard times can breed success in other areas of life?

Today December 27, 2017

December 27 2017, a day before my 27th wedding anniversary. It has also dawned on me that I am not on the financial and economic level of stability that I expected to be at this point in my life. I have always secretly believed that by the age of sixty, I would be financially able to retire. Nowhere within those plans did I foresee being involved in a multi-million- dollar lawsuit against the state of New York. I definitely never foreseen that I would be suing the state of New York for libel, slander, defamation of character, and defamation of business reputation. I also never foresaw the filing of a complaint against the sitting Chief Justice of the New York state Appellate division, Third Department, and against a sitting New York State Supreme Court Judge. Thus far, one of the most important lessons learned in my life is that one should always expect the unexpected, and one should never say never. Another important lesson learned is that one should never give up. No matter what the odds are against you or however powerful your opponent may appear to be. At this point in my struggle, no one knows what the outcome of my story will be. But what I can guarantee is that I will never stop or discontinue my fight. After all, how can one effectively defend others if they're unable to defend themselves? It is my hope and desire that my children will stand ready to defend themselves whenever it is necessary and no matter who the opponent may be.

CHAPTER 27

THE PETER PRINCIPLE OF CORRUPTION – ABSOLUTE POWER CORRUPTS ABSOLUTELY

A famous man once said that absolute power corrupts absolutely. I would make a slight amendment to this saying and add that any real power would or could breed and lead to corruption at the highest level that it has access to.

Like the Peter Principle which states that individuals will rise to their level of inefficiency. This saying basically means that an individual in most situations would continue to rise or progress until the attainment of a level at which they can no longer efficiently perform. Power would seek to breed corruption at the highest level that it or whoever holds power has access to or has the ability to influence.

On November 21, 2017, after not receiving any assignments from the Tioga County Court system for approximately three months, I called the court to inquire why I had not received any assignments. I was then informed by the court clerk that she received a phone call from the New York State Office of Court Administration directing them to stop assigning any new cases to me, but that I should be allowed to complete any existing case in which I was/am currently assigned. I immediately made various phone calls, and eventually spoke to the judge who made the call to the Tioga Court and informed her about what I was told by the Tioga County Court clerk. The Broome County Court judge immediately told me that she was instructed to do so by the Chief Judge of the New York State Appellate Division because, according to her, I was owing money to the court system for work performed in Broome County, New York. The reality of the story is that currently I have in my possession over one hundred assigned and completed cases for which I am being owed by both Broome County and New York State. This statement by the judge is not only false, but without merit.

Now let's recall the course of events that occurred since October 11, 2012. In October 2012, my name was removed from both the assigned council panel in Broome County and the Law Guardian Panel/Attorney for the Children Panel in the Third Judicial Department of New York State. I was falsely accused of overbilling the County of Broome and State of New York while I was a member of both aforementioned panels. These false allegations and accusations resulted in a one-week jury trial in which I was found not guilty of all charges, resulting in all charges against me being dismissed. Since October 2012, I have not performed any legal services for the County of Broome and or the Law guardian Panel/Attorney for the Children Panel in the Third Department of the State of New York. One would believe that with this knowledge any reasonable and fair- minded person would've recognized that both the State of New York and the County of Broome were wrong, and that the allegations were and are unfounded. Except for two key pieces of information that were not mentioned. First, the Chief Judge of the Appellate Division, Third Department was among some of the responsible parties for all of the allegations made and the eventual trial and was trying her best to clear her name while creating the appearance that wrongful conduct had occurred. Second, she was retiring at the end of December 2017, so this was her opportunity to clear her name while seeking her final revenge. She retired about four years before her judicial term had expired.

It is my belief that she is trying her best to create or foment her legacy, even if it means destroying the name of any innocent person. This situation is a perfect example of what can and usually does occur when small minded people find themselves in high places. That is the Peter Principe at its very best.

My response to the conduct of both judges was a complaint to the Judicial Committee on ethics in the State of New York. On December 4, 2017, I submitted an ethics complaint on those two judges to the Committee of Judicial Standard. Below is a verbatim copy of the exact complaint sent to the Committee of Judicial Standard. The names of the two judges are removed for the purpose of retaining anonymity and also to increase or not distort from the credibility of my complaint.

December 4, 2019
State Of New York
Commission on Judicial Conduct
61 Broadway, Suite 12
New York, NY 10006

Re: Complaint Against
  Hon. Karen K. Peters and
  Hon. Molly Fitzgerald

Dear Sir/Madam:

On November 21, 2017 after not receiving any assignments from the Tioga County Family Court, or any other criminal courts within the County of Tioga, I called the Clerk of Tioga Court to inquire if I was still on the Tioga County Assigned Counsel panel since I had not received any assignments since August, 2017.

I was advised by Jill, Judge Kane's secretary, that that the Tioga County Court Clerk's office received a phone call from Hon. Molly Fitzgerald instructing them to allow me to complete whatever ongoing assigned case I was working on, however no new or additional case should be assigned to me.

I then called the chamber/office of Hon. Molly Fitzgerald and informed her about what I was told by the Tioga County Court Clerk's Office, and inquired about what was told to the court. Hon Fitzgerald's response to me was, "Do not shoot the messenger." She went on to say that she received a call from Hon. Karen K. Peters instructing her to make such a request because I am owing money. I informed Hon. Fitzgerald that I am not owing money to anyone, and also asked her to send me something in writing concerning what was told to her by Hon. Peters and the action that was taken.

Hon. Fitzgerald agreed to write me such a letter, but said I would not receive it until after the Thanksgiving Holiday.

On Monday 27, November, 2017 at about 12:00 p.m. Hon. Fitzpatrick left a message on my voicemail stating that "Hon. Coccoma will not be issuing a writing regarding you not getting assignment in Tioga. He has refused to do that." As earlier stated I never asked for Hon. Coccoma to write any letter to me. I asked that Hon. Fitzgerald write me a letter stating what was told her by Hon. Karen K. Peters.

Background Information

In October 2012 the State of New York wrongfully obtained a warrant and seized 344 of my clients' files. I was wrongfully accused of overbilling the State of New York and County of Broome for law Guardian/attorney for the Children cases and assigned counsel cases. These wrongful accusations resulted in a one week jury trial in Broome County Court from October 19, 2015 to October 23, 2015. I was acquitted of all charges by a Broome County jury. Some members of the jury were shocked by the actions of the state.

After my acquittal I wrote to the following Judges:

Hon. Lawrence K. Marks, Chief Administrative Judge, NYS office of court and Administration, and Hon Michael Coccoma, 4 ESP, Suite 2001, Albany, NY 12223.

I expressed to them how shocked and surprised I was by the actions undertaken against me by the State of New York. In that very letter to both of the above mentioned judges I respectfully asked for the following?

1. Rescind their letter/order, hence paying me for all work performed and unbilled

2. Reinstate me to all panels on which I was member, and

3. *mail a copy of the letter/Order so stating to me.*

To date I have received no response from either of the above mentioned judges.

On December 15, 2015, approximately two months after my acquittal, I mailed a copy of the very same letter that was earlier sent to Hon. Lawrence K. Marks, and Hon. Michael Coccoma to Hon. Karen K. Peters.

About one or two weeks after mailing my letter to Hon. Karen K. Peters, I received a letter (it is my recollection that this was a faxed copy of the letter) from Mr. George Danyluk in which he mentioned overpayments made to me by the law guardian program and Broome County. Mr. Danyluk's letter to me was also dated December 15, 2015. The same date on my letter sent to Hon Karen K. Peters. I have in my possession about one hundred (100) completed and unbilled cases, together with at least one hundred open/incomplete cases that were being worked on, that were reassigned to other attorneys in the assigned counsel and law guardian/attorney for the children program.

Retaliation/Reprisal and abuse of Power

My last date doing any assigned counsel and law guardian cases for the county of Broome and the State of New York was October, 2012. All accusations and charges were litigated in a Jury trial in which I was acquitted of all charges. The current actions of Hon. K. Peters and Hon. Molly

Fitzgerald constitute total disrespect for the Jury System and holding themselves out to be over the law.

Neither Hon. Karen K. Peters nor Hon. Molly Fitzgerald had the courtesy to inform me of their actions to call Tioga County and ordered them to stop assigning any more cases to me. Had I not called Tioga County to inquire about my status on the assigned counsel panel, I would never have known of their unethical conduct. I am unaware whether Tioga County was the only jurisdiction contacted by the judges.

The actions of Hon. Karen K. Peters, Hon. Molly Fitzgerald and Hon. Cacomma violate the civil and criminal laws of the State of New York which they took an oath to God and Citizenry to uphold. The actions of judges who knowingly and brazenly violate the criminal and civil laws without responsibility or consequence cannot be condoned. The commission with this knowledge should appoint a special prosecutor so that the taint of the bad conduct of the judges does not besmirch the commission itself.

I am kindly asking the commission to investigate their actions. Thank you for your assistance in this matter.

Please provide me with a copy of your written actions to protect the integrity of the system of law from the knowingly bad acts of multiple judges at multiple levels.

History provides too many instances of the evil brought upon humanity when the law is knowingly and willfully ignored by those in authority. Take a step back and decide what history will be written when it is noted that you were aware of knowing bad acts by multiple levels of judges and what steps you took to stand for truth and justice. Those actions will echo down the halls of justice decades after our hearts stop beating.

Yours respectfully,
John D. Cadore, Esq.

It should also be noted that the above actions by both judges occurred after my first court appearance in which New York State was sued for among other things, libel, slander, defamation of character, and defamation of business reputation. Since filing my lawsuit against the State of New York, this is not the only retaliatory action taken against me. However, I was forewarned that once legal actions officially began, there would be such retaliation against me or to paraphrase a certain individual, "You would soon be facing retaliatory actions by individuals attempting to protect their names while having no regard for yours." My experience, if anything, should demonstrate that "members of the judiciary are no different from members of the public at large".

Individuals Placing Themselves Above the Law

The actions of the aforementioned two judges, by making phone calls and requesting that certain actions be taken, amounted to placing themselves above the law. There was a trial by jury in this matter. According to the verdict of the jury, they saw no wrongdoing on my part. Who gave two judges the power and authority to override a jury's verdict? The action of those two judges constitutes a total and complete abuse of power. By their actions, they have said that the decision of the jury shouldn't be recognized if you do not like the verdict.

There is an old saying, "No one is above the law." Those two judges, by their actions, have said that they're above the law, and that whatever they decide to do is in fact the law. This is a demonstration that absolute power indeed corrupts absolutely.

CHAPTER 28

NOVEMBER 14, 2017 – A DAY NEVER TO BE FORGOTTEN – WHEN IT RAINS IT POURS

It was approximately 5:30 PM on November 14, 2017 when we (my wife and I) were returning from a small town in upstate New York called Masonville. Masonville is approximately forty-five minutes north of the city of Binghamton, New York. We were returning from Masonville Town Court travelling south on Route 81 about twenty miles away from Binghamton New York, when my vehicle, a 1997 Ford Ranger pickup truck, was rear-ended by a driver I believe was travelling at approximately one hundred miles per hour. My vehicle was travelling at approximately sixty miles an hour. I was travelling smoothly and uneventfully towards the city of Binghamton when I heard a loud bang, and my vehicle was thrust forward. It was a total surprise. Thankfully, we were both wearing our seatbelts, which immediately tightened when we were hit. In my over forty years of driving, this was absolutely my first time ever experiencing such an incident. It was a direct hit from behind. The front of the other vehicle directly ran into my vehicle. It was a direct head-to-rear accident. I have heard of and seen head-to-head accidents before where two vehicles collided head on, but I have never observed a head-to-rear accident until that night.

Both vehicles were totaled, meaning that they were considered to be totally lost. I did not observe the driver of the other vehicle, but I was told by the police that his car was badly damaged, and there was debris from the accident all over the interstate. According to the female police officer, the driver in the other car was not injured. I was also informed by the police officer that portions of his vehicle could be found in a small ditch just off the (freeway) interstate. My 1997 Ford Ranger is a very sturdy old-time or traditional vehicle that I believe is built from fiberglass. It's my belief that had my vehicle been a newer model, the accident would've been much worse. My vehicle was built very strong and it showed. The other vehicle was a modern 2015, 2016 or 2017 built/made vehicle and it showed. The damage to the other vehicle was much more serious than the damage to mine . Additionally, it's also my belief that were I not an experienced driver with extensive driving experience, including tactical military driving courses, the outcome of the accident might have been much different.

After the initial first hit and shock of a major collision, one must have the clarity and vision to allow the vehicle to run for a reasonable distance before applying the brake. This would accomplish two goals. First it will prevent a cluster of vehicles on the fast- moving interstate. Secondly, it allows the driver to maintain control of the vehicle after the initial (hit) collision. My vehicle was declared to be a total loss by both the New York State Troopers and by the insurance company, but because of my love of this particular vehicle, I am seriously considering repairing it and returning it to working condition for future use. It's my belief that the other vehicle in the accident is beyond any hope of repair.

I must give all credit to the almighty God for being here today to be able to write about this event. It was not a pretty sight or great experience. I did not see the driver of the other vehicle involved in the accident because, although the accident occurred at approximately 5:30 pm on November 14, 2017, it was very dark outside and that portion of the interstate had no street lights. This accounted for a very serious and dangerous situation, and I was not in the mood to add to the existing level of danger by getting out of the vehicle to locate the driver. It is believed by many that every situation or event happens for a reason. I am asking myself what is or was the reason for this car (crash) accident? There was no carelessness on my part, so what could the lesson be?

My Home in San Antonio, Texas

After my first discharge from the U.S Army in December 1982, I used my military benefits to purchase my first home in San Antonio, Texas. I had this home for over twenty years, and it was fully insured at all times. The home was destroyed by fire set by an arsonist and despite many conversations with the insurance company, they refused to pay for the home. The insurance company found a loop hole, which was wrongful, to avoid paying for the home. This situation occurred in the midst of my political investigation and my political trial that occurred between 2012 and 1015. Adding to the dilemma here, I was unable to leave the State of New York to attend any legal proceeding in Texas during that period. I was prohibited by the court from traveling outside of New York State during that period. Now after having mentioned this event and the actions of the insurance company, how many people would believe that United States Automobile Association (USAA) was the insurance company that would partake in such wrongful conduct? USAA was founded to serve military officers and their dependents. However, its membership was later extended to include all branches of the military and their dependents. I became a member of USAA in 1985 or 1986 when I was a Reserve Officer Training Core (ROTC) cadet at The University of Texas at San Antonio.

I attempted to obtain representation in San Antonio, Texas for this matter, but I quickly realized that USAA was way too big and had accumulated way too much power and most law firms within the State of Texas did not want to be on USAA's bad side. They were happier being a friend of USAA than an opponent. I obtained an evaluation of my case against USAA from a New York State Fire Liability company who quickly informed me that USAA had no basis to not honor their insurance policy.

While I do not want to sound like I am sourgraping, I can definitely say with utmost certainty that all of the legal matters that I was involved in within the last eight years, I was absolutely in the right. However, USAA's actions were very shocking to me. I have served honorably in the U.S. Army, the U.S. Army Reserves, the Texas Army National Guard and the New York State Army National Guard. I had expected much better from USAA, but why should I? After all, USAA is an insurance company whose primary interest is its bottom line.

CHAPTER 29

THE NEW REALITY OF MY CHRISTMAS AND NEW YEAR'S VISITS TO TORONTO, CANADA

Prior to October 2012, on all of my extended visits to Toronto, Canada, I would carry between six (6) and ten (10) of my clients files with me, to either review them, or complete assignments in those files that needed to be completed before my next court appearance, or to prepare for upcoming trials. Today, it's a much different situation. Instead of working on case files as was my regular custom in Toronto, today, December 29, 2017, I am writing chapters for my soon to be published books. This is the fourth chapter that I've written since my first visit to Toronto on December 23, 2017. I have traded my case files for written chapters in my manuscripts.

Which is the most productive use of my time: working on case files or writing chapters in my soon to be published books? The answer to this question is uncertain. The ultimate answer would be left to the imagination and conclusions of the individual readers. My guess is that intellectual readers would probably conclude that writing chapters for soon to be published books constitute a better and more productive use of one's time, whereas more pragmatic and practical readers may conclude that working on upcoming court cases is a more productive and rewarding use of one's time. My guess is that there is no right or wrong answer to this question. It is wholly subjective and depends on the various values each individual places on the short run, the long run, and the very long run. By the short run, I'm referring to time periods of up to six months; the long run refers to the time periods from six months to twenty- four months, whereas the very long run refers to the time period beyond twenty- four months.

The answer to this question may also vary remarkably among members of different countries. The answer will be based on the value systems of the individual societies. It is my belief that the more intellectual cultures and societies will be more accepting of book writing, whereas the more practical, hands-on nations will be more favorable towards reviewing case files for upcoming cases. Of course, there will be those countries in the middle of the spectrum. I would go out on a limb and predict that the people of my home island are more enthusiastic about my book writing. Already, I have gotten book inquiries from a handful of them. All demonstrating enthusiasm and readiness to read what I have to say and mostly my story. It is my belief that my military background would render my upcoming books more appealing and may increase the level of credibility and enthusiasm my publication will receive.

My greatest regret is for my books and publications to bring condemnation and disdain to the U.S and its way of life. This is not my intention but being a very realistic person, I know there are those that would use my publications to paint the U.S in a very unfavorable light. Although this is a serious concern of mine, I, in no way, would refrain from writing about the true stories and events because of the various reactions it will receive. The basic truth is that no one can keep a good man down and likewise, a good and strong nation would eventually regain its prominence and respect amongst societies and nations. The reality is that individuals that love the U.S would continue to love it, whereas individuals that dislike the U.S would find additional reasons to increase their dislike and hold disdain for it. Thus, in the very long run, very little, if any, will change.

Capitalism would eventually prevail because people are primarily concerned with their own survival and well being. It is a well established fact that most Americans view themselves as failed capitalists that one day will find their time to shine. A failed capitalist is someone that has not yet accomplished their capitalist dream but hopes and dreams for accomplishing that dream, is sooner rather than later. For this reason, it is strongly believed by many that communism and marxism views or viewpoints would probably never blossom or become popular in the United States.

Most people somewhat believe that one day they will be the winner of a big lottery. To me, the biggest characteristic for the continuous growth and expansion of capitalism is hope; hope that one day they or we will "hit it" and become somewhat wealthy. Hence, it is my belief that in order to diminish the spread of capitalism, one must be able to diminish the hopes and dreams of individuals.

CHAPTER 30

THE BLOCKADE BY THESE COUNTIES

Prior to October 2012, my legal practice consisted of clients and court assignments from primarily three upstate New York counties. They were: Broome County, where I currently reside; Tioga County; and Delaware County. Occasionally, I would handle a case or represent someone in Cortland County or Chenango County.

Today, my client pool and assignment from those three counties have almost extinguished. This reality on one hand can be seen as sad, but on the other hand, it represents and demonstrates the temporal nature of mankind. It reinforces the old saying of ebb and flow of business and life as a whole.

Nothing would ever last forever, and things would never remain the same. The question one should ask oneself is, how would my behavior or actions be different when circumstances change? What would your new priorities be? To a certain extent, there is a level of joy that occurs during such a circumstance because it allows you to see individuals for what and who they really are. Now

I know that no one wants to experience bad times or difficult economic circumstances. But it is in bad times or difficult economic circumstances that real and true growth really occurs.

Although I do not believe that my father, who is now one hundred years of age, is happy with my experiences the last five or six years, but to some extent, I also believe that this is a good learning and growing experience for me.

Poverty: The Real Cause

Unlike what many may say or explain as being the main cause or causes of poverty, it is my belief that the real cause of poverty is lack of vision. This is believed because my experiences have taught me that individuals who look for instant gratification will have the tendency to remain poor. One may inquire of me why such a statement should be made? As I mentioned earlier, my experiences have taught me; for example, I can recall calling many individuals providing day labor to make small repairs on certain buildings and houses for me. The majority of those individuals would be of no assistance because in their estimation, they're not being paid enough now. Just imagine if one's financial or economic situation were to suddenly change. What is the most unlikely reaction or inclination from the person who was hiring those unlicensed individuals to provide day labor? An educated guess would more than likely be that such a person when faced with a sudden increase in wealth or financial standing would no longer seek to employ any unlicensed Individuals, unless those unlicensed individuals were reliable during the lean years. He or she would primarily utilize licensed contractors because a license would guaranty the quality of his or her work and because one can most likely locate and recall the licensed individuals were the work not properly done during the first instance. Hence, no longer seeking the services of unlicensed workers.

Although nothing is ever always true, it's my belief that lack of vision is most likely the primary reason for generational poverty. Some may argue that this theory is false because of the undocumented laborer/immigrant situation. If anything, the undocumented laborer situation would make my theory hold true because the vast majority of undocumented workers, once they obtain legal or proper documentation, would become legal residents, whether by attainment of green cards or work permits over a period of time, eventually would join the nation's middle class. This is because the vast majority of undocumented workers that come to the U.S or any other country are seeking a better way of life. Additionally, they are usually very dependable and very hard working. In the vast majority of instances, they are much better workers than local citizens. That fact has repeatedly resulted in undocumented workers, once documentation is obtained over a period of time, would usually become employers of the natural born U.S citizens and their children.

However, research has repeatedly shown that the children of the once undocumented workers that are born in the U.S or in whatever country they migrated to, do not perform as well as their formerly undocumented parents. The children of the once undocumented workers usually do not have the drive, the determination, and the heart as their once undocumented parents. The end result is usually relinquishing some of the prosperity and gains made by the once undocumented parents.

Again, one may ask, why are you so confident making such statements? My answer is that as an immigrant myself, this has been the reality for many immigrant families. This situation is also true for immigrant families that legally immigrate to the U.S from other countries. The drive and determination usually diminish with each generation. This is what many immigrants or people refer to as "Americanization".

CHAPTER 31

INNOCENT UNTIL PROVEN GUILTY – FACT OR FICTION

It is well established within the United States Constitution and the New York State Constitution that an individual is innocent until he or she is proven guilty in a court of law. It is also a well- established principle within the law that once an individual is found "not guilty", reasonable and good faith efforts must be made to make that innocent individual whole. Those my friends are well- established tenets within the rule of law.

The question remains, do those supposedly sacred tenets also apply to the legal profession? Or simply put, is the legal profession or are some members of the legal profession primarily judged as being above the law? Are judges exempt from following the law? Based on recent experience and observation of the daily workings of the Third Appellate Department, one may be left with very little choice but to conclude that some of the judges of the third Appellate division within the State of New York are of the belief that they are above the law. Could it be that those very judges are now programmed to believe that they are entitled and part of that entitlement is placing themselves above the law?

Could it also be that those judges only adhere to a jury verdict when they agree with it? And conversely, disagree and disrespect the verdicts of the jury when they don't fit their plans or schemes? Over the last eighteen months or so, it appears that this is perfectly true. Or could it also be that those very judges felt so privileged that whenever their kingdom is threatened, such threats are met with the utmost retaliation. This judicial retaliation can only be described as judicial abuse of power. It is also believed that such abuse of power is somewhat widespread and goes unreported and unchecked because the majority of people under their jurisdiction are either afraid to report it for fear that nothing will be accomplished or done, thus subjecting themselves to additional abuse. Is it also true that others do not know what can be done about it, or if anything can be done about it? This problem can rightfully be described or explained as the tip of the iceberg scenario.

The author is in no way saying that people who are the subject of judicial abuse are weak and indecisive. Instead, self- preservation and, in some cases, lack of knowledge in the vast majority of cases are the reasons for inaction.

My Initial Court Appearance: My Civil Law Suit Against New York State

August 24, 2017 was the date of my initial court appearance in my civil suit against New York State. It was the equivalent of a lynching. The judge appeared and conducted the hearing as if she was a party to the case. It was totally biased towards the state. The judge even went as far as telling the Assistant Attorney General to file a motion to dismiss the case.

The problem here was that according to New York law, the judge was absolutely wrong on all points of law. The judge went as far as suggesting that my case was frivolous. Her actions were the equivalent of an employee of the New York State Attorney General's Office. In fact, she was more biased against me than was counsel for the defense. After observing the judge's behavior and the way that she conducted the initial hearing, I immediately said to myself, "Thank God that there is an appeal process". She conducted the initial hearing not as a judge but as an employee working for the New York State Attorney General's Office.

CHAPTER 32

HONESTY ALWAYS TRUMPS DISHONESTY. TRUTH ALWAYS TRIUMPHS OVER LIES

Throughout the Bible, it is consistently or routinely stated that the truth will always prevail over lies, and that lies could be sitting on a throne while truth is seated or placed on a scaffold but truth will always prevail. However, truth will always triumph over lies. The bible has routinely stated that the days of Satan are numbered and that Satan is only a loser.

I've always believed every word written in the bible, and I have always known it to be true, but it is somewhat astonishing how quickly those words can come true. My father has routinely told me that not only does what goes around comes around but one will be amazed at how quickly it comes around. How does all of the above apply to me and fit into my case?

I stated in my first and second books that I was totally innocent of all accusations made against me, both by Broome County and the State of New York Attorney

General's Office. Most astonishingly, both of the public officials that were instrumental in making false allegations against me were forced to leave public office in disgrace. The Broome County Executive, a major player in this matter, is now a disgraced public official after pleading guilty to one count of official misconduct for wrongfully appropriating public moneis for her personal use. She was arraigned on three counts of official misconduct and entered a guilty plea on one count. That Broome County executive was fined $1,000 with a guilty plea. Tonight, the 7th of May 2018, while briefly watching television, there came a story about New York Attorney General Eric Schneidermann. According to the story, the New York State Attorney General, Eric Schneridermann, has physically, sexually, and emotionally abused at least four women. Shortly thereafter, maybe twenty minutes or so later, a news story broke that the New York State Governor, Andrew Cuomo, has asked the New York State Attorney General, Eric Schneidermann to resign because of the physical, sexual, and emotional allegations against him. Again, about ten minutes or so after that precious announcement, there was a news story that the New York State Attorney General Eric Schneiderman had resigned because of accusations of physical and emotional abuse against multiple women.

According to the news as it broadcasted over channel 19 on cable television, multiple women gave multiple statements about physical, sexual, and emotional misconduct they experienced at the hands of the New York State Attorney General, Eric Schniedermann. According to the news, some of those women reported their abuse at the hands of the then New York State Attorney General to other people during the periods that they were under the abuse.

Tonight, at 11:17 PM on May 7, 2018, I can safely report that two of the individuals who were primarily responsible for bringing false charges and making false accusations against me have left public office in public disgrace. These occurrences supported what is written in the Bible when it said, "Lies could be seated on a throne, and truth seated on a scaffold, but the Truth will always prevail." To this statement, I would undoubtedly or wholeheartedly say amen. I know this is true because Jesus said it and also because I have experienced it.

Without becoming too repetitious, let me quickly recall my experience in Broome County Court on 08/14/14 at approximately 1:30 PM. As was stated in my first book, when false charges and accusations were being read against me, suddenly a soothing peace and tranquility overtook me. It was like an out-of-this world experience; a complete and total peace engulfed my body both inside and out. It was the type of peace that this world cannot give you. It was total peace and tranquility, like a divine peace.

Based on my experience in the Broome County Courtroom on August 14, 2014 at around 1:30 PM, I was not surprised that two of the individuals that were instrumental in making false allegations against me have met their demise. Although I am not wishing or hoping that any individual would or should be falsely accused, it is my hope and desire for many people to experience the peace and tranquility that I experienced on 08/14/14 at approximately 1:30 PM at the Broome County Courthouse. To me, both Broome County Executive and the former New York State Attorney General have similar traits and one thing in common. That is, both individuals would easily step on whoever they perceive they can step on to further their political careers. Their cravings for power and political prominence would lead them to abuse the political office and betray the public trust. I experienced it firsthand. They both have another trait in common, the truth was rarely in either of them.

After reading chapter one of this book, one might be led to believe that I am happy about the political demise of both the Broome County Executive and the former New York State Attorney General. However, this is not the case. They are two flawed individuals that provide examples of what public servants shouldn't undertake or partake in. A good public servant is one that tries to lift people up and not tear people down and especially not to further their careers on the backs of innocent and hardworking people.

CHAPTER 33

MY CHURCH ATTENDANCE SINCE OCTOBER 11TH, 2012

Prior to the incident whereby my law offices were searched by officers sent by the New York State Attorney General's Office, I attended my parish church very frequently. It's my recollection that apart from being a member in the men's group at my church, my church attendance was very regular; it could've been every Sunday with few exceptions. I can recall attending mass on Sundays then, with the company of my wife, visiting the homes of children for whom I was appointed by the State of New York to represent as a law guardian or attorney for the child. In short, a law guardian is an attorney for the child. In many cases, when more than one child is involved, the law guardian also acts as the children's attorney. On many occasions, I would travel to different counties, visiting the homes of different children.

On a few occasions, I would, sometimes on Sunday after Mass, visit various clients. Of course, my Sunday visits were rare and only happened when the case was due in court early on Monday morning, or there was a motion being argued in which I believe that effective representation would require a Sunday visit.

Today, it is extraordinarily difficult for me to conceive of regularly the notion of attending Sunday Mass at the very church and in the very parish in which I have been a member for numerous years, approximately twenty years to be exact. It is even harder for me to accept that individuals from my very parish church who have known me and my family for such a long time to partake in such wrongful and vindictive actions. Of course, maybe I should not be surprised. After all, Jesus is the Alpha and Omega, the Creator of this world, and even Jesus was put to death by the actions and encouragement of wicked church-going men. Hence, why should anyone treat me differently? I am just an ordinary man.

Most surprisingly and in some cases scary, is that the judge that signed the warrant authorizing the search and seizure of my clients' files is also a member of my church and parish who I regularly would meet or see at that very church. A few of the people that are involved in spreading false rumors against me are also members of my church and parish. Very often, the abovementioned facts lead me to ask the question: is God present in that congregation? Or were we worshipping a false Jesus? My conclusion is that God is available to everyone and for everyone who seeks him. God is also omnipresent; therefore, he can be worshipped from any location. Therefore, no reason exists to believe that one must attend that particular church or any particular church to have a relationship with God.

Another question that frequently came to mind is whether my church congregation and the time spent worshipping were merely a social gathering. Maybe I am naïve, but it would have been very clear and very easy to find out that my office was not involved in any wrongdoing or wrongful conduct. Third, what role, if any, did being a black man of African descent and an immigrant play in the actions of the judge and other members of the church and parish?

Currently, I have no definite answers to those questions but would be very curious to find the answers. After being found not guilty of any wrongdoing, the state with the aid of some individuals (some judges) were working overtime to cover up their wrongful and illegal conduct. It is my belief that they are doing so in order to protect their reputations. From approximately August 2014 to today, the New York State Ethics Committee has been conducting an investigation into my case. It is unbelievable that such a simple ethics investigation is taking over four years to complete. Many individuals have voiced their opinion that the ethics committee is taking a long time to respond because the committee is trying to protect and cover up the wrongful actions and conduct of some of their friends. Many people are also of the opinion that the entire situation was caused because of jealousy combined with racism. I have not entertained any such thinking since I have never been jealous of anyone and racism is a new or somewhat new phenomenon to me. Racism was never a part of my daily upbringing in the Caribbean. It may be quite unbelievable to many but racism is still a somewhat new reality to me. It is something that I may never be able to fully comprehend or understand. Many have expressed to me that the basic tenets of racism is to keep some individuals at a lower level on the social ladder. Hence, attempting to exhibit dominance in many avenues of life over them. As stated earlier in this chapter, despite living in the United States for so many years, the idea of racism is still a somewhat foreign notion and concept to me. It is my belief that whatever one man can do today, another man can and will do tomorrow. My father, who passed away on April 1, 2018 at the age of one hundred, once told me that it takes an ass to make a nuclear bomb, and a jackass to use it because once any nation uses such a weapon on another nation, it's only a matter of time before that same nuclear bomb, or a similar one, will be used on them.

Today, I can remember my late father saying to me "Not only what goes around comes around, but one would be surprised at how fast it will come around." My father went on to explain that he arrived at that conclusion after his one hundred years of living on this Earth.

I stated earlier that my father was over one hundred years old when he passed away. The uncertainty surrounding his exact age is due to the fact that during that time period, it was not uncommon for children's birth to be registered many years after they were born. Most of the people in the villages where my father was born were either farmers, fishermen, or both. Children's birthdates were of low priority to them. In many instances, a child could have been registered as being born several years after their actual birth. Such child's registration was commonly done by a neighbor or friend that happened to be going to the city on the day in question. Very often, registration of a child's birthdate was not done by their natural mother or father, and, very often, the child was given the birthdate of the day that neighbor happened to be going to the city in which the child's birth was to be registered. This should not be construed to mean that children's birth in some parts of the world is not important, because it is. However, in many developing nations of the world, the actual date of birth of a child is not given top priority. Most priority is given to feeding and clothing the family.

During my father's memorial service, one woman said to me that's her father who is still alive at the age of ninety-four told her that my father is at least one hundred and ten years old because when he, this ninety-four-year old man, was a very young boy, my father was already a grown man. According to that ninety-four-year old man, he has known my father during his entire ninety-four years of life. This belief about my father's age is shared by many of the elderly people in the village and in all of the surrounding villages.

CHAPTER 34

THE COMMISSION ON JUDICIAL CONDUCT

Today, June 8th, 2018, I called the commission on Judicial Conduct to inquire of the status of a complaint filed against the two judges. One of the judges complained about was the former Chief Judge of the Appellate Division, Third Department in Albany, New York. That particular judge retired in December 2017. However, before her retirement as the Chief Judge of the Supreme Court Appellate Division, Third Department, I was informed by a Broome County Supreme Court judge that the retiring Appellate Division Judge from Albany, New York called her, the Broome County Supreme Court Judge, and instructed her to call certain courts and tell them to stop assigning any cases to me because I owe money to New York State and Broome County.

May I remind everyone that such actions by the various judges occurred after a jury trial that found that I was innocent of all charges made against me? Many believe that this was retribution and retaliation by the retiring New York State Appellate Judge for exposing their corruption. It was retaliation because I filed a lawsuit against New York State seeking damages for libel, slander, defamation of business reputation and defamation of character. My law suit alleged seventeen different counts, and seeks damages for, among other things, libel, slander, and defamation of character. This included damages of business of business reputation and personal reputation. Concerning my phone call to the New York State Commission on Judicial Conduct on June 8, 2018 about the two aforementioned judges, I was informed by the commission that there was no record that a complaint was filed against those two judges on February, 26, 2018. I know that this statement is false because approximately two weeks earlier I called the commission to inquire about my complaint about those two judges and was informed by the office manager or by a worker at the commission's office that she personally had delivered my complaint to an investigator whose job it was to review the complaint. That worker also advised me to write a letter to the commission inquiring of the status of the complaint. I was also informed by that commission worker that the investigator, to whom the complaint was given, in keeping with the rules and regulations of the Judicial Commission on the judicial conduct should have written me a letter acknowledging receipt of my complaint. This, however, never occurred. No letter was received from the commission acknowledging my complaint. Additionally, no reply was ever received acknowledging receipt of my letter dated May 25, 2018 inquiring about the status of my complaint against those two judges.

After being advised of having no record of my complaint on June 13, 2018, I resubmitted the very same complaint filed on February 26, 2018. But on this occasion, the complaint was addressed to a particular individual. The complaint was faxed to the commission, and on the very same day, I called the commission's office and inquired of the individual to whom it was addressed, whether the complaint was received. To this question, I was answered in the affirmative. It was my intention to keep checking on the status of the complaint every two weeks.

I am not drawing any conclusions, but I am asking myself whether certain judges are being protected by various investigations at the commission.

The Structure of the New York State Court System

Within the State of New York, there are many lower courts. At the bottom of the New York court structure are town and village courts. Within the town and village courts, one doesn't have to be an attorney admitted to the bar in New York State to be a town or village judge. There are also city courts. In most or all city courts within New York State, a judge is required to be a licensed attorney. The next court in the New York State hierarchical system is the county court. Every county court judge is required to be a licensed attorney/lawyer and in good standing with the bar. Above county courts is the Supreme Court. Unlike most states, where the Supreme Court is the highest Court in the State, the supreme court in New York State is a Court of General Jurisdiction and isn't the highest court in the state. The next court in the state hierarchy is the Supreme Court, Appellate Division. There are four Supreme Court Appellate Divisions in New York State. The City of Binghamton and the County of Broome sit in the Third Appellate Division in New York State. The next court in the hierarchical chain is the New York Court of Appeals, which is the highest state court in New York State. The aforementioned court system does not include any federal court that sits within the State of New York. Within the federal system, we have the district court, which is basically a trial court, and the Federal Court of Appeals.

This brief introduction into the New York State Court System is only meant to provide an overview to the readers who may not be familiar with the New York State Court System. This system is somewhat different from the court system in many other states.

CHAPTER 35

MORE GOOD NEWS

Shortly after returning from my father's funeral in Grenada, a small island in the Caribbean, I received a letter from an attorney stating that one of my tenants sustained an injury on my property due to dangerous conditions. I seriously questioned this assertion because about one month before the alleged injury, the property was inspected by the government and found to have no defects. The property withstood an in- depth inspection conducted by a government property inspector that is known to be one of the toughest inspectors and most difficult in the business. I seriously doubt that the alleged incident occurred or, if it occurred, took place on my property. But because my properties are fully paid for and I have no mortgages or notes on any of them, it is not mandatory to carry liability insurance. The house in question is fully insured.

However, for a landlord to protect him/herself from liability, there must be a clause in the lease strongly encouraging the tenant to purchase their own rental insurance. In this case, any liability incurred by the tenant will be covered by their rental insurance policy.

After losing a few nights of sleep over the alleged incident, I went and reread my lease with that tenant, and of course, there was a paragraph in the lease encouraging or strongly recommending that the tenant should purchase rental insurance in the event of any unforeseen liability.

However, the biggest revelation came after about four weeks after receiving the letter from the attorney. The property in question was fully insured against all perils and liabilities, including liabilities involving the tenant or any tenant residing therein since 2013. Throughout all of my legal problems, there were no breaks in the coverage of the insurance policy. When this policy was initially purchased in 2013, it was done via the use of direct withdrawals from my checking account. Largely unknown to me, throughout all of my trials and experiences, this policy and means of payment was never altered or interfered with.

The property was fully insured, and I never knew it or, because of the many ups and downs (mostly downs) over the last six or so years, I had forgotten about it. What a coincidence.

Pertaining to the rental property agreement or lease, a landlord cannot order a tenant to purchase rental insurance because only a court of law or a tribunal has that authority.

This situation is still ongoing, but all of my worries brought about by this injury allegation are no longer serious concern of mine. Anyhow, having full insurance coverage on that property, it is my belief that the tenant isn't entitled to any recovery for alleged injury. The reasons for holding this belief are threefold: first, the tenant stated that she wanted to relocate or move to a different apartment or home because she was on a medication that rendered it very difficult for her to walk up any type of stair or stairway; second, the house, only one month earlier, had passed a very in-depth rental inspection in which all four corners of the house were inspected and passed all inspections; third, the tenant was strongly encouraged in the lease to purchase rental insurance to protect herself from any unforeseen liabilities. However the tenant did receive a settlement from my insurance company, and I am very happy for her. I do wish her well.

CHAPTER 36

WRONGFUL GOVERNMENTAL CONDUCT

The road to recovery for wrongful acts committed against you by politically appointed or elected officials would, in most cases, result in a long and winding road to recovery. The reason being that political officials and/or people elected to public office, in most cases, are the vast majority of instances, incapable of admitting wrongful conduct. Admitting wrongful conduct from their perspective is most likely seen as risking their political careers. Additionally, in most cases, the officials has displayed a persona that they are and have been straight shooters. Hence, to admit to the citizens who elected them to office that this is not the case is often perceived or viewed as very threatening to their careers.

Additionally, most public wrongs committed by elected representatives or career government officials or public employees are most often wrongfully and deliberately committed in an attempt to foster or boost their political careers or political standing. Committing those wrongful acts could result in political payoffs for those who commit them. Of course, that is usually the case if such public officials or career civil servants are not caught for their wrongdoings. In most instances, wrongs are committed by political figures or career civil servants because of personal or political gains to be realized should their wrongful deeds go unchecked, unrealized, or unnoticed by the public at large.

However, there are other types of wrongs committed by elected public officials or career civil servants. These wrongs, in most instances, are prurient in nature. Such acts are not usually committed for political advantages or furtherance of one's political career. These types of acts are usually carnal in nature and are driven by the lusts of the flesh.

One example of an elected official committing wrongful acts to promote their political career was personally recently experienced by me during the period I began writing this book. After my acquittal in my political criminal trial, I wrote a letter to the then chief judge of the Third Department of the Appellate Division of the Supreme Court of the State of New York expressing my shock, surprise, and dismay at the actions of the State of New York, especially judicial officials in the Appellate Division of the Third Department. Shortly thereafter, that very same chief appellate judge of the Third Department of the Supreme Court of the State of New York made a phone call to a Supreme Court judge in Broome County instructing her to remove my name from Assigned Counsel Panel in the courts overseen by them. All of these actions were undertaken without notice to me, by either from the Chief Judge of the Supreme Court Appellate Division Third Department or Broome County Supreme Court Judge ordered to take the wrongful action.

I became aware of the actions when I called a certain court and inquired from the Court Clerk why I was no longer receiving calls and assignments from them. According to that court clerk, "they were instructed to not assign any new cases to me". The court clerk informed me of what was told to them by the Broome County Supreme Court judge. The court clerk expressed her astonishment that I had not been informed of the actions taken by the Supreme Court Justice. This is a perfect example of people abusing the law and holding themselves to be above the law.

Since that occurrence, the chief judge of the Appellate Division has retired, and I have heard that the Supreme Court judge who did the dirty work and wrongful act of removing me from the panels had gotten a promotion and will soon become a justice on the Third Department Appellate Division in the year of 2020. This is a perfect example of my initial statement that some wrongful conduct committed by public officials for the political purposes of advancement and promotions in title. The job titles carried by the bad actors here all carry the same base pay. The action to gain a higher office is just a stroking of the ego of the office holder.

One may be tempted to ask how do you feel about what happened to you when the wrong doers seem to be climbing the political and social ladders? To that I would reply what I was told by my late father, "Son, it is much better when people do you wrong, than when you do others wrong." So to answer the question, I would say, "I feel much better that they are the ones committing the wrongful acts than if it was myself committing those wrongful acts."

CHAPTER 37

MY PART-TIME EMPLOYMENT

Still suffering the after effects of the financial impacts heaped upon me by and my legal practice by the unscrupulous politicians and their lieutenants on December 16, 2019, I accepted employment with a law firm headquartered in a different city in New York State. This position was of short duration. Once again, this experience highlights the importance of education, especially within the minority communities. Education is the primary or main way forward to economic, political, and social advancement for minority communities throughout the world. There is an old saying believed by many, "It is not what you know, but it is who you know." My experience has led me to primarily reject that old saying. Who you know is very important and can sometimes serve as a tailwind pushing one forward but according to my experience, what you know is at least ninety percent more important than who you know. There is another old saying, "It's not who you know, but who knows you." I must confess that my experiences over the past seven years have rendered both of these sayings somewhat untrue. The reality is in troubled times, most of the people one thought were their friends would disappear.

I must confess that maybe both of these sayings, "Not what you know, but who knows you," is not given much credibility because it is my natural instinct to hold my future or my progress in my own hands as much as possible. Now I am fully aware that things never go as planned and that God is the ultimate decision maker. My late father, on several occasions, said to me, "Son, man does not share bread." According to my father, if men were allowed to share bread, he would take the majority for himself, his family and his friends. Thus, according to my father there is a higher power that is ultimately responsible for how your bread is distributed and to whom it is distributed to.

Another reason why my belief in these two old sayings is so trivial or minuscule is also because of international employment and alliances. Let's say for example that the nation of Chad, West Africa, is in need of a nuclear scientist or a nuclear physicist. Only a nuclear scientist or nuclear physicist is qualified for that job. One can either obtain the requisite qualifications for most jobs by either education or experience. One must obtain the requisite education to become a nuclear physicist or scientist, or one must have the requisite experience to perform the job. For the most upper echelon of specialized employment, the requisite qualifications are obtained by both education and experience. Those who you know may be of little or no importance in obtaining that job. I can safely say that no one would be employed as nuclear scientist solely based upon "who one knows or who knows him or her."

One's level of experience and education would be the primary qualifications considered when making an offer to fill that position.

Back to my part- time employment with the law firm. The primary reason, the only reason for obtaining that part- time position with that law firm is because of my education and work experience. I did not know anyone in that law firm, and I was not asked for a reference. It is my belief that being a solo practitioner for over 20 years was enough. I briefly worked part- time for that law firm but maintained my private practice and private office.

Within a few weeks, my first book will be published. It is my ability to express myself in a written format and my experiences that have led me to write all of my books. Once again, the old saying, "It's not what one knows, but who one knows" has been thoroughly debunked. Please do not interpret my reasoning to mean that it is not good or advantageous to know people and have connections. Those things are complementary. However, the key is educating one's self and being qualified for whatever opportunity or opportunities would present themselves to you.

CHAPTER 38

ROAD BLOCKS IMPOSED BY JUDICIAL PERSONNEL AND STATE EMPLOYEES

After being victorious in the political criminal prosecution, I once again refocused on restarting and rebuilding my legal practice. This effort was suddenly met with harmful acts and bad conduct by the same individuals and organizations that had been responsible for the failed political criminal prosecution. They were attempting to make a statement. That statement was: We are above the law and are not bound by the verdict of the jury of your peers. We have the ability to do whatever we so desire.

Litigating the very same facts of the case which was heard by a jury and dismissed, the non- elected officials of the Office of Court Administration began a new campaign against me. Some of the vindictive actions taken against me were now focused on my license to practice, as attorney grievance complaints generated by high- ranking state employees and state officials that were embarrassed by their failed political prosecution. Phone calls were made to the courts that assigned work to me and were instructed to stop giving me work. All this occurred without any notice to me and an opportunity to be heard.

The questions I repeatedly ask myself is: to what extent has the color of my skin influenced the wrongful conduct? And, what role, if any, does my national origin play or influence their actions? Other questions frequently asked and considered are: How much of their actions are due to those players attempting or trying to keep or maintain their respective jobs, titles and positions of authority to continue to exert in their sphere of influence?

Please remember that all of this is being done to a veteran with many years of military service. Without any notice to me or any knowledge by me, the former Presiding Justice of the Supreme Court of the Third Department Appellate Division placed a phone call to Supreme Court in Broome County, administratively someone who is bound by rules of employment to follow the orders of one's superior and directed that justice to make a call to other Office of Court Administrations employees and telling them to stop assigning new cases to me. The question remains, how many other courts were called and requested to stop giving me assignments of work?

As may have been noticed in my earlier paragraph, I said former Presiding Justice of the Supreme Court, Third Appellate Division of The State of New York engaged in such clearly improper and wrongful acts. That justice retired five years before her appointed term had expired. The dramatic irony in this dilemma is that the Broome County Supreme Court Justice who followed the wrongful orders of the now retired Presiding Justice has now been promoted by the Office of Court Administration to the Appellate Division, a huge step up in honor and prestige among legal profession. The direct link between her taking actions which were knowingly wrong at the request of her administrative superior probably was the precise political capital needed to obtain the higher rank, title, and authority that an appellate court judgeship commands.

President Donald J. Trump is a politician. The position of a judge is studiously and laboriously legally defined to be one who applies the law as it exists to the facts that are presented. The role of the judge is not to create facts out of whole cloth to meet the requirements of the law that the judge wishes to apply to the fact pattern. It is my opinion and position that judges should be held to a higher standard than other employees of the state and even of the elected members of the legislature.

Based upon the past seven years, it is my conclusion and belief that even if the allegations against the President are proven to be true, he should not be removed from public office. This issue should be decided by the voters. The issues of national politics are not the subject of this book but rather much more local conduct of officials sworn to uphold the law.

CHAPTER 39

THE AFTER EFFECTS OF FALSE ALLEGATIONS IN FINANCIAL DEALINGS

Since being falsely accused of over billing for legal work performed, it has had a chilling effect on accepting cases where financial payoffs are directly tied to the case. It has left a bad taste in my mouth for also accepting specific cases directly related to the recovery of money. For example, I received a position as a collection attorney working on behalf of a somewhat large national organization with branches conducting business in several states. I received the offer and was willing to give it a try but the thought of dealing directly with financial matters of people undergoing financial difficulties, I was never very comfortable with.

A friend once said to me, "Once bitten, twice shy." Based upon my experiences, I would conclude that there is a lot of truth to this saying. I received another job offer from a law firm in another state. This job would have also entailed pursuing financial recovery from debtors in several different industries and in several different states. Because of my experience over the past seven years, I am not and was not very enthused or enthusiastic about accepting any of those positions. It is my belief that because of my admission to the bar in several different states, law firms in the area of financial recovery were very attracted to me. A law firm once contacted me to inquire whether I am admitted to the bar in the State of New York, the State of Connecticut and the State of New Jersey. When I answered yes, the law firm then wanted to know if I would be willing to get admitted to the State of Pennsylvania. This was a law firm that was specialized in national collections and financial recovery. Currently, I am admitted to practice of law in four States, and I am very satisfied with that; unless or an until a truly extraordinary opportunity presents itself that would be require me to be admitted to a fifth state, I am not very interested in doing so. I am much more interested in being admitted to the practice of law in a different country than being admitted to practice law in a fifth state. I am very amenable to the practice of law in a different country instead of being admitted to the bar in a fifth state.

CHAPTER 40

THE PARADOX OF MY RELIGIOUS LIFE

It is very often said that many people will frequently attend church services during the bad times or down times in their lives and for many people, the bad financial times of their lives. However, it is often also said, in fact I heard it from a preacher's mouth, that during the good times or economically prosperous times church membership normally declines. For me, this has been the exact opposite. During the financially prosperous times of my life, church membership and church attendance were the cornerstones of my life. However, during the financially lean years, my church membership and participation significantly declined. This is not because I stopped believing in God during my economically lean years but because certain individuals that played a significant role in the governmental wrongful conduct and wrongful governmental actions promulgated against me were members of my parish church . Though my church membership significantly declined during my economically lean years, my relationship with God significantly improved. It is my belief that I now have a good and strong relationship with God. It is very difficult for me to attend weekly or daily mass in a church where I am not comfortable with trusting members of the congregation. Partaking in God's service should not be done with an untrusting heart.

One may rightfully ask, what role does forgiveness play in the Christian life? The answer to that question is that forgiveness is the cornerstone of Christian life. But even after forgiving others, one must be careful because Satan is like a thief in the night, lying in wait for those he can devour.

I frequently hear pastors say that people usually attend church during the bad times of their lives and disappear or stop attending during the good times. For me, the exact opposite is true.

However, whenever I visit my family or in-laws in different cities or countries, attending mass is usually one of my top priorities. I attended Christmas Eve or midnight mass in Toronto, Canada for Christmas 2019. One of the most significant observations during the two occasions I attended mass there during late 2019 and early 2020 was the reduction in numbers of people attending the church service. I have made that observation because in prior times and prior years when I attended church services at that very same church, the church building was full to capacity, and I can recall many people standing throughout the service because of no available seats. This time it was totally different. There were many empty and available seats. Could it be that the pastor's observation that people usually attended church services during their bad or hard times but stop attending during their prosperous times is really true? If that is indeed true, what is the reason for it?

Could it be that many people in Toronto and the Caribbean have left the Catholic faith for other denominations? Could it be that there are more services offered at different times during the day? Could it be that many of the parishioners have died? Is it that the total population has decreased? All of those are reasonable answers for the significant decline in church attendance recently observed.

CHAPTER 41

WHEN IT RAINS, IT POURS

Thus far, the year 2020 has started with many significant disappointments. There is an old saying that a bad beginning brings a good ending. If that saying is indeed true, then great things await me in the latter part of 2020.

My first major disappointment in 2020 is a ruling by the Honorable Kevin Dooley in a tax foreclosure proceeding involving one of my rental properties. Despite paying my property taxes and I had until February 15, 2020 to pay any outstanding property taxes, the County of Broome wrongfully foreclosed on my property. Several motions were made to the court highlighting their mistakes; nevertheless, the court refused to reverse its decision. I was left with no choice but to appeal the case to the Supreme Appellate Division, Third Department. The case is currently pending before the New York State Court of Appeals.

The questions to be asked here is, was this retaliation or payback for the State of New York losing their case against me? Is it payback for me suing the State of New

York? Or, is it a combination of both? Binghamton, New York and Broome County, New York are both relatively small places. The author has his suspicion and belief but would like to keep them private. After reading my other two books, the conclusion on this matter would be left to the reader.

CHAPTER 42

CONCLUSION: BEHIND ALL DARK CLOUDS IS A SILVER LINING

There is an old saying that tough times do not last, but tough people do. There is another old saying that goes whatever doesn't kill you only makes you stronger. It is my experience that both of the aforementioned sayings are true.

Today, as I sit writing this paragraph, I have two job offers in two different states. As I sit writing this paragraph at 6:55 p.m., I am open to many possibilities. Finally, it seems and appears that the commencement of a new chapter in my life is at hand. However, whatever the outcome may be, it is my desire to continue, or should I say, start writing books. My goal is to publish at least one book a year for the rest of my life, or for the next ten or fifteen years.

My new goal of an annual publication may seem too many to be coincidental and to others, it may be predestined. I can recall at the age of about ten or eleven, hearing about the death of a famous author.

This writer predominantly wrote novels considered by many to be westerns. Westerns are novels whose primary characters are cowboys and Indians.

I can vividly recall that upon learning of this western novelist's death, I immediately asked God to help me to become a successful author. However, I did not only want to be writing to a small portion of the population or to members of a particular country. I asked God to give me a worldwide audience and to allow my books to be in the homes of many people all over the world, and especially people residing behind the countries traditionally referred to as The Iron Curtain. This dream I believe would very soon become a reality. At this point in time, it is unknown if I will ever publish my first book. But I must admit that as of today, I have begun writing four different books, none of which are fully complete or published. Hope springs eternal, so it's my desire that another one of my boyhood dreams/desires will soon become a reality. One of my many boyhood goals was to become an attorney. A goal that was realized over twenty- eight years ago.

www.ingramcontent.com/pod-product-compliance
Ingram Content Group UK Ltd.
Pitfield, Milton Keynes, MK11 3LW, UK
UKHW022215230426
12048UKWH00016BA/849